I'll Take My Disease Rare Please

My Journey with Fibrosing Mediastinitis

Rebecca Lalk

Copyright © 2015 Rebecca Lalk.

All rights reserved. No part of this book may be used or reproduced by any means, graphic, electronic, or mechanical, including photocopying, recording, taping or by any information storage retrieval system without the written permission of the publisher except in the case of brief quotations embodied in critical articles and reviews.

WestBow Press books may be ordered through booksellers or by contacting:

WestBow Press
A Division of Thomas Nelson & Zondervan
1663 Liberty Drive
Bloomington, IN 47403
www.westbowpress.com
1 (866) 928-1240

Because of the dynamic nature of the Internet, any web addresses or links contained in this book may have changed since publication and may no longer be valid. The views expressed in this work are solely those of the author and do not necessarily reflect the views of the publisher, and the publisher hereby disclaims any responsibility for them.

Any people depicted in stock imagery provided by Thinkstock are models, and such images are being used for illustrative purposes only. Certain stock imagery © Thinkstock.

ISBN: 978-1-5127-0739-7 (sc)
ISBN: 978-1-5127-0740-3 (hc)
ISBN: 978-1-5127-0738-0 (e)

Library of Congress Control Number: 2015912763

Print information available on the last page.

WestBow Press rev. date: 8/18/2015

This book is dedicated to my husband, Timothy Lalk, for loving me at my worst, for standing forever by my side, and for being my support and my strength. Thank you for your extremely hard work and all of the sacrifices you have made in order to be at all of my appointments and procedures, as well as doing whatever necessary to provide for our family. Thank you for making me laugh throughout some of our darkest days and for helping me to make the most of our situations. Thank you for encouraging me and helping me to push forward not only in life but also throughout the process of my writing. Your confidence in me has helped give me the courage to step out of my comfort zone and follow through with completing this book. Thank you for making the life that I was told I would never have filled with love, faith, laughter, exciting experiences, and sincere happiness. I love you always and forever. I am blessed.

Acknowledgments

Most importantly, I want to thank You, God, for giving me a second chance at life, for loving me unconditionally, and for never leaving me when I felt I had strayed too far. I thank You for putting the right people in my path and for experiencing circumstances and hardships that turned into amazing blessings and led me back to You. Thank You for giving me the strength and courage to write this book. Thank You for giving me a second chance at improving my relationship with You in order to do the best I can to live life the way You intend for me to do.

To my mom and dad, Steve and Vicky Arends, who have shown by example throughout my whole upbringing that by putting God first, anything is possible. You have taught me to be strong in faith and determined to do anything I set my mind to, to pray, and to believe. Thank you, Mom, for always listening to me, providing encouraging words, and being my voice when I didn't want to fight my battle any longer. And thank you, Dad, for always being at the appointments with me, knowing I can rely on you for anything and everything, and especially for your strong hugs to comfort me in my time of need. The faith you both have is inspiring. Thank you for encouraging me to never give up.

To our oldest daughter, Skyler Shoemaker, for always making me smile with your wild sense of humor and for being my inspiration from the very beginning of this journey. Thank you for being able to joke and make light of whatever situation or physical testing I am going through. Thank you for always being able to recognize and reach out to help, especially when you know I am not feeling well. And to our other children Nathan, Leah, and Asher, thank you for being the other part of my sunshine. I love you all, always and forever.

And a special thanks to my sister Michelle Runde, my sister-in-law Sarah Arends, my cousin Julie Routh, and my dearest friend Dusty Perkins for listening, laughing, and being a shoulder to cry on throughout this whole journey we call life. God has blessed me with amazing family and friends, and I know I can count on all of you to be there with me through the good times and the bad.

Thank you to the rest of my family as well as Tim's family for all of your love, patience, compassion, and understanding, as well as your willingness to help out with whatever we might need. A big thank-you to my sister-in-law, Brenda Nederhoff, and mother-in-law, Debbie Lalk, for helping out tremendously with the children so that Tim could accompany me to my never-ending doctor appointments.

Thank you to our small group, including Dave Lindley, for helping Tim and me to come up with the perfect title based on our personality, as well as doing the photography for the book. Thank you to Dave's wife, Angie Lindley, for being so supportive and passionate about creating the perfect format and cover design for my book as well.

Thank you to all of our friends, my coworkers, and especially my supervisor, Jan Heidemann, for accommodating my needs in order for me to continue to be successful with my job. Thank you to our church community and my FM family for all of your support, prayers, and encouragement.

To my amazing medical team at the University of Iowa Hospitals and Clinics, including but not limited to Dr. Youness and nurse Deb, Dr. Hornick, Dr. Rossen and nurse Pam, as well as interventional radiology along with all of the techs and other nurses I see throughout my routine testing. To every doctor and nurse I have come across, answers or no answers, thank you for being a part of my medical adventure and for doing all that you can to help me!

> She is clothed with strength and dignity;
> she can laugh at the days to come.
> Proverbs 31:25

Unable to hold my breath any longer, I pulled my head up from under the water. It was a beautiful summer day; what better way to spend it than sitting outside, soaking up the sun, and listening to the birds chirping off in the distance?

I was out in the backyard relaxing in Skyler's baby pool, counting how long I could hold my breath underwater while she napped inside. It was just something silly I was doing to pass the time, a mild amusement on an otherwise peaceful day.

Just as I was about to dunk myself under for another attempt, I heard the phone ring. In a rush, I jumped out of the water and dashed into the house, hoping simply to catch it before the ringing woke Skye. I had no idea how drastically this one phone call would forever change my life.

At least, not until I heard my doctor's voice on the other end.

For most of my life, I had been relatively healthy. There had never been any broken bones or surgeries, and I had always been active. Until now, the only blip on my medical radar had been my diagnosis with juvenile diabetes my junior year in high school.

I was seventeen when it happened, young enough to not fully understand the severity of what I was dealing with. It was my mom who had broken out in hives at the news, instantly worried and knowing I would be facing a lifetime of watching my diet and monitoring my blood sugar levels. Not to mention I would need to give myself daily injections, needles now a necessity for keeping me alive.

That was also the first time I had known my dad to cry, as Mom would later tell me he had left my hospital room to go out in the hall for that very reason. Even my younger brother, Ryan, and my older sister, Michelle, seemed worried. *Really?* I thought. *What's so bad about this? I mean I lost fifteen pounds in three days!*

To my teenage mind, that was a silver lining if ever I had seen one.

I struggled off and on with managing my diabetes those first few years, just wanting so desperately to be "normal." I even went as far as having my boyfriend or friends check their blood sugar for me, just so I could use their results to keep my mom from knowing if I had skipped a shot. It wasn't that I enjoyed the repercussions of missing injections; it was just that giving myself four shots a day felt ridiculous. I didn't want to be that girl. I didn't want to be sick.

Of course, I quickly learned that diabetes was not a joke or a diet plan. It only took a few instances of passing out for me to realize that if normality was what I wanted, I had to follow the rules. And as much as I hated it, I eventually tried to make the most of it. Mom had always said God blessed me with a sense of humor so that I could get through the trials in life. In this case, that turned out to be true. When I couldn't hide the illness, I laughed about it.

Turn everything into a joke, and it can't hurt you, right?

A few weeks before this call that would turn my world upside down, I had gone to the doctor as a formality more than anything. I didn't feel all that terrible, but I had been dealing with this cough that just refused to go away. I assumed it was the lingering effect of some cold and that I might need antibiotics to clear it all up. The doctor had seemed to be of the same mind-set, sending me for a chest X-ray just to make sure I didn't have pneumonia.

But now, he was on the phone saying he wanted me to come in for more tests. Those X-ray results had just made their way across his desk. There was a mass on my right lung.

"Is it cancer?" I asked, torn between my need to know and my desire to continue living blissfully unaware.

"Possibly," he replied.

I hung up the phone and sunk down to the floor, waves of shock washing over me. I was only twenty-seven years old. This didn't make sense. I wasn't even a smoker. My beautiful little girl, Skyler, had just turned two. Her father and I were in the middle of a divorce. So much of our relationship was damaged beyond repair. But there had been relief in our separation as well: a promise of a life I could reclaim and begin living as the person I knew I was. The person I wanted my daughter to see me as. Everything I did, every ounce of my being, was about a commitment to her. My little girl. My baby. The light of my life.

Cancer was not an option. It just ... wasn't.

I was referred to a local pulmonologist. My parents were there by my side, accompanying me from appointment to appointment, just as they had when I was first diagnosed with diabetes.

A biopsy was ordered first. Doctors made the incision through my neck, leaving an unseemly scar about an inch long. I joked about that, of course, pretending the scar was the most devastating part about this whole ordeal. But when the results came back undetermined, I was referred to Dr. Wait, a general surgeon at Covenant hospital in Waterloo, Iowa. His suggestion was that he simply go in and remove the mass. As far as I was concerned, getting whatever this was out of me sounded just fine. So the date was set for me to have a thoracotomy.

I had accepted Jesus into my heart at an early age, but I had drifted. There was a period when going to church, reading the Bible, and keeping God as my main focus had become less of a priority. In truth, that was partially why my marriage had faltered. God was nowhere to be found in our union. And without God being the center of our relationship, all of the hurt and obstacles that we faced could not be repaired.

Several months earlier though, before all this cancer business started, I began attending my parents' church in Cedar Falls,

Iowa. This is where I grew up, and the general area where I lived my entire life. I was determined to recommit myself to my faith. So of course, I made sure that I went to church with them the Sunday before my surgery. I sat in the pews and prayed. I pleaded with God for everything to be okay, revealing the depths of my fear to Him while I was still in a stage of laughing it off to everyone else.

We walked out of church together and headed to my car. But then suddenly, my parents seemed to stop for some reason. I had just started reaching for the door when I realized my baby brother, Ryan, was sitting in the driver's seat. Turning around in an instant, I caught sight of his wife, Sarah, now standing beside my parents.

The tears erupted from my eyes before I could gain any kind of control. My brother was in the military, currently living in Texas, and we didn't get to see them as much as we liked. But he and Sarah had come home for my surgery. They were here for me. I couldn't remember the last time I had felt so loved, supported, and grateful.

A few days later, I underwent my thoracotomy, telling myself that the mass would be removed and this nightmare would be over. Instead, the nightmare was only beginning. Even just waking up from surgery, I knew that I had been naïve. I had convinced myself this was no big deal, but a thoracotomy is a major surgery known to involve a great deal of pain during recovery.

I found that out the hard way. I had never experienced anything like this. It was excruciating. Giving birth to my daughter had been a breeze compared to the pain I was now in.

I had twenty-four staples going from the middle of my back down to my right lower side. At the end of the staples, there was also a wound about the size of a quarter through which my breathing tube had been inserted. It hurt to breathe now. It hurt to move. And Skyler being only two years old made this even harder. She wanted to be in my lap forever, and I certainly didn't want to deny her that. But I would cringe in anticipation of the pain every time I saw her running toward me, arms outstretched and asking for a cuddle. How do you turn that down though? How do you say no to your baby girl who just wants to love you?

The worst part was that Dr. Wait had not been able to remove the mass. He explained that it was hard like cement and impossible to remove and it had several new blood vessels called collateral veins that should not be there. He insisted he had never seen anything like this before. The surgery was stopped early because, as he told me now, if he had continued with removing the mass, he might have hit one of those blood vessels simply as a result of not knowing where they all were. And if that had happened, I would have bled to death.

Dr. Wait also said that my right lung was pushed up from what appeared to be scar tissue. He had tried to push it back down but had little success on account of how solid the scar tissue was. Again, he said that in all of the surgeries he had ever done, this was something he had never come across.

But he had been able to get enough tissue to send to the Mayo Clinic. And while I was recovering, still battling the searing pain at my incision site, I was finally given a diagnosis.

Fibrosing mediastinitis.

And just like that, life became so much more difficult. Things had already been tight, with me trying to navigate the waters of parenting through a divorce. I had been working hard to make ends meet all on my own, and now I had to figure out how to somehow juggle work, Skyler, and all of my appointments at once. I spent forty hours a week working as direct care staff with individuals who had mental illnesses and physical disabilities. Meanwhile, I feared that I might one day soon wind up in their shoes.

I found myself back in Dr. Wait's office after the thoracotomy for a follow-up appointment. He began by saying, "The good news is it's not cancer."

Neither of us knew then how wrong he was, that in this case, cancer would have been preferable. In my wildest dreams, I would never have imagined the day would come that I would find myself wishing it *had* been cancer. That it had been something where there was at least hope.

Fibrosing mediastinitis, or FM for short, is a very rare disease. At the time of my follow-up, that was all Dr. Wait could tell me. There were no doctors in the area who had ever even heard of this condition, which was why I was immediately referred to the Mayo Clinic in Rochester, Minnesota.

I walked into that huge waiting room only to turn around and walk right back out. I was sure I must have been in the wrong place. The room was full, and almost every patient in there was at least seventy. They were all wearing oxygen masks, carting their own tanks, and getting around on walkers. I looked at the door again, secretly praying that I had made a wrong turn somewhere. But my heart dropped when I realized that no, I was exactly where I needed to be. And so I made my way back into what seemed to be the geriatric ward. I was not even yet thirty. This had to be a joke, right?

I sat waiting for my name to be called, haunted by a single thought. *What am I doing here?*

Once finally seated in a patient room, the doctors began to explain to me what I was dealing with. But just like when I had been a kid being diagnosed with diabetes, the severity of this situation seemed to be lost on me. I couldn't wrap my head around what they were saying. It all sounded like a foreign language.

They explained that FM is a very rare and life-threatening autoimmune condition. At the time, there were only about two hundred people in the United States who had been diagnosed with this disease. The doctors informed me that it was caused by histoplasmosis, an infection that produces normal cold and flulike symptoms. The infection itself was fairly common, but an immune deficiency could lead to severe complications that resulted in the development of FM.

The medical industry's understanding of how histoplasmosis develops has grown some over the years, but this was 2002. There were really just theories back then. The doctors suggested it might have been the result of exposure to bat or bird droppings in areas where there was a lot of dirt or dust being stirred up. The Mississippi River and Ohio River valleys were also potential breeding grounds for the histoplasmosis fungus. The theory was that this fungus produced spores in the air, leading to a common infection. Most people exposed would just get a cold. But I ... I was one of the (un)lucky few to develop something much worse.

I had gone on a lot of family vacations growing up and we toured caves, like the Carlsbad Caverns in New Mexico. Without knowing for sure, I wondered if I could have gotten it from there. We had also spent some summers at Lake Pepin on the Mississippi River, where histoplasmosis was apparently common. As a family, we racked our brains trying to figure out when I could have become infected. But there really was no way of knowing for sure.

I just kept thinking, *I'm going to die because of bird poop. How bizarre is that?*

I was so focused on the question of *how* this had happened that my brain seemed to protect itself from the inevitability of what was to come. But that didn't stop the doctors from trying to explain it to me.

The most dangerous aspect of FM is calcified fibrosis, or scar tissue. In very rare cases like mine, the body overcompensates with this scar tissue to fight off the histoplasmosis fungus. It is essentially an autoimmune reaction—the body basically attacking itself in an attempt to get rid of something else. Unfortunately, that scar tissue then begins to block and cut off major organs and vessels. The area most affected in my body at the time was my right lung, which was apparently only functioning at one-fourth the level it should have been. This explained the lingering cough I needed a chest X-ray for in the first place.

Everything in front of me was a blur when I heard the doctors explain that this disease had a ten-year prognosis and that there was nothing they could do for me.

As I walked out of the Mayo Clinic, all I could think about was the fact that I would be dead by thirty-seven. Skyler would be no older than twelve when she would lose her mommy. I wouldn't see my daughter drive a car for the first time. Or graduate high school. I wouldn't be there for her when she had her first heartbreak or when she walked down the aisle toward the love of her life. I would never hold my grandbabies.

I was going to miss so much, so many of the life events I had relied so heavily on my own mother for. And suddenly, it all sank in. The severity of this. The reality of the situation I was now up against. It hit me like a semitruck just as I was getting into the front seat of my car.

It was there that I collapsed beneath the grief and tears, knowing only that there was nothing acceptable about leaving my little girl behind.

Once home, I threw myself into Internet research. Much to my frustration though, I barely found any information at all about FM. It was like this ghost disease that no one had ever heard of. Not even the Internet could guide me.

The best resource I managed to come across was a personal web site started by a couple of individuals who were afflicted by this condition themselves. I began poring over everything they had ever posted, quickly feeling overwhelmed by all that I was reading. It wasn't just their stories; there were also stories of other people with FM. People just like me who had scoured the Internet for answers and landed in this exact same spot.

Most of what I read was devastating. The few people who had posted were young when they were diagnosed, like me, yet so many of their stories seemed full of despair and heartbreak. They talked about being in excruciating pain on a daily basis. They shared their struggles with breathing at night and the point in their journeys when they had finally succumbed to the necessity of oxygen tanks. I read story after story, unable to ignore this one shared truth: every one of these people sounded absolutely miserable.

I could feel myself sinking into a depression, reading these stories that seemed to offer little to no hope. I had introduced myself on the site and shared my own story at first, but I found myself pulling away as the weeks wore on. I was mostly asymptomatic, while many of those posting online seemed to be in pretty rough shape. I told myself I was nothing like them. I needed there to be some sort of separation between them and me, something that differentiated us. Because I didn't want to be them. I didn't want to become them. Their stories scared me too much to imagine myself in their shoes.

If only I had known then what I know now, that this group would later be there to encourage and support me during my most difficult times fighting this disease. That I would eventually come to offer them hope and light as well.

Everything happens in its own time, I suppose.

Because there was no cure, and no treatment options to be heard of, I was basically released back into normal life after that initial Mayo Clinic appointment. The only thing they wanted from me was an annual checkup, purely to monitor the progress of the disease.

The thing was I was feeling mostly healthy and symptom free. So it didn't take long for the diagnosis to become this thing in the back of my head that I just didn't think about very often. I was a single mother with a busy life; I didn't have a ton of time to focus on something that didn't really seem to be affecting me. Not to mention Skyler was still so young. So of course, I hadn't really talked to her about any of this. Which meant that in my day-to-day life, it wasn't a topic of conversation.

It took a little longer for the shock to wear off for the rest of my family. But they eventually "forgot" that I was sick. I was living like nothing was wrong with me. I even started to believe that maybe the doctors had misdiagnosed me. I certainly didn't feel like somebody who was dying.

Still, I kept up with my annual appointments until 2005, when for the first time ever, treatment options were offered to me. I was basically given three choices. The first was an antifungal treatment thought to reduce the accumulation of scar tissue. Unfortunately, due to my diabetes, this drug was counted out as an option right from the start. It would have negatively affected my blood sugars too much.

The second option was like a cancer treatment. Basically, due to the fact that this disease was so rare, doctors seemed to be just grasping at straws in order to try to stop the progression of whatever was growing inside me. This treatment consisted of chemotherapy, so there was a risk of dangerous side effects, without a lot of guarantees that it might help. Not to mention chemotherapy would certainly inhibit my ability to have future children.

The third option was nothing more than a trial. So far, the study participants had experienced terrible side effects and shown no real progress. The doctor was pretty quick about going over all of the options with me. He said that because I was still asymptomatic and all of my testing was stable, the unknowns associated with each of these options probably wouldn't be worth it for me at this point in time. He just had to review them with me, simply because there had been no options for treatment at all previously.

The fact of the matter was that with fewer than two hundred people diagnosed with this disease, the treatment options were simply a guessing game for doctors and patients alike. Had I been actively sick, I might have been more open to taking on the risks some of these treatments carried. But I wasn't. And I still wasn't totally convinced I even had this disease.

Of the three options the doctor gave me that day, none of them really felt like options at all. He even admitted to me that none had shown especially promising results, and all came with major drawbacks.

Option one was automatically out because of my diabetes, and the reality was I didn't see the trial as something I wanted to do—not with the way my doctor had described it. Just in skimming over the information, he wasn't sure if I would even be a considered candidate.

My symptoms were still very mild. All I had was a minor cough, and most days, I didn't even notice that. I loved Skyler. I loved being a mom. I had always wanted four kids—a big, flourishing family. I wasn't totally ready to give up on that possibility yet, and certainly not for a treatment that offered no guarantees and had zero success stories so far. It just seemed like so much to give up, when I was otherwise living a relatively normal life.

My faith had me wanting to believe there would be other options, other possibilities, if I could just wait a little while longer. After all, advancements were already being made, just in the three years since I had been diagnosed. So who was to say more couldn't be just around the corner?

I decided that for the time being, I was going to remain on the same path I had been on—putting my trust and faith in God. I was hoping and praying for something more concrete to present itself before I pursued any treatment options.

I suppose I wasn't ready to fully embrace this as my future just yet. The doctors had no guaranteed treatment for me, they knew nothing about this disease, yet they wanted to tell me how many years I had left to live. I couldn't help but feel they might be wrong. Because let's be honest: doctors aren't always right. I wasn't ready to give up on anything in my life just yet. And I reasoned that, disease or no disease, tomorrow was never a guarantee for any of us. I was going to live my life to the fullest, as if I didn't have anything wrong with me, because it didn't feel like I did.

―――•―――

In 2007, five years after my initial diagnosis, I was still relatively symptom free. There was always that occasional cough to contend with, but other than that, no one would have guessed that I wasn't completely healthy. Even I sometimes fooled myself into believing the whole FM nightmare had been just that—a nightmare. One that I had clearly already woken up from.

Perhaps it was my naiveté, or maybe that unshakable desire I still had to be "normal," but I had stopped attending my annual appointments after 2005. It just felt pointless to continue going after I had turned down all the treatment options offered to me, and nothing about those appointments ever made me feel any better. It seemed easier to just keep living my life as though nothing were amiss, assuming that I would know when the time came that I could no longer ignore the ticking time bomb inside my body.

Skyler had just celebrated her seventh birthday. She was getting older and developing into her own little sassy self. We had a small apartment in Waverly, Iowa, and lived right across from the high school, where Skyler loved to go and play on the tennis courts. I was still working for the county, but my job now involved me working seven days on and then having seven days off. My ex-husband and I shared custody, alternating weeks, so my work schedule was absolutely perfect for our situation. It allowed me to fully focus on Skyler during the weeks I was with her.

Of course, the weeks that I didn't have her were harder. I didn't want to admit it, but I was angry. Angry that I was sick and angry that there seemed to be little I could do about the impending inevitability of what this disease would do to me. I didn't like being alone with my thoughts. I didn't like the opportunities to think about that lingering cough and what it meant. And sitting at home just left me to worry about Skyler and to wonder if I was doing a good job as her mom, to wonder if it would be enough for her to hold onto once

I was gone. Most of the time, I was pretty convinced I was making a mess of all of it. To quiet my thoughts, I started going out with my coworkers at night during the weekends Skyler was with her dad. And when we went out, we drank. We partied. I dulled those sad and angry thoughts in ways that were probably less than healthy.

While I was still attending church with my parents, I really wasn't allowing God any more time in my life. Secretly, bitterly, there was a part of me that felt like if He was going to cut my life so short, I wasn't going to devote any more of it to Him.

A few weeks after her seventh birthday, Skyler woke up one morning and began begging me to take her for a bike ride. So I got my running shoes on and loaded her up with kneepads and a helmet before we took off out the door. She was trying to ride as fast as she could on her *High School Musical* bike as I ran effortlessly beside her. This was a regular routine for us, *our* routine.

We began on our normal route, but we had just made it up the street when I was hit by this sudden coughing attack. It was bad. So bad that I had to stop, sure I was going to throw up right then and there. I stood under a tree, bent over with my hands on my knees. I was trying so hard to catch my breath, but I could not stop coughing. The pressure in my chest was tremendous.

Eventually, we were able to make our way back to the house, where I was finally able to regulate my breathing once more. Skyler was sad and kept begging me to go back outside with her, but I was nervous. I knew I wasn't in the greatest shape, but I also knew there was no reason I shouldn't have been able to run two blocks. I had always been very active, ever since high school, and Skye and I spent a lot of our time playing volleyball and basketball. We were always swimming, and even golfing or going across the street to play tennis. We were forever outside as a pair, Skyler always happiest when surrounded by fresh air. Sure, I wasn't an Olympic athlete, but I was fit enough.

I should not have been coughing up a lung after running two blocks.

Still, this was me we were talking about. The same girl who had once convinced others to scam her blood sugar tests so that she could get away with skipping very necessary shots. I wasn't about to let this one incident define me. I pushed it to the back of my head. I went about my daily routine and pretended it hadn't happened at all. That it didn't mean what I *deep down* knew it meant.

Unfortunately, my body wasn't as willing to let me pretend the inevitable away. I began experiencing horrible headaches, soon accompanied by ongoing and intense chest pressure. Plus that nasty cough refused to dissipate.

I finally went to my family doctor, but nothing was wrong according to him. All of my levels and tests came back normal. He never even mentioned the possibility of my symptoms being related to FM. And I chose not to remind him. Instead, I just continued trying to live my life, determined to keep pretending. Only that became harder and harder to do. I kept telling myself the symptoms I was experiencing were a result of being out of shape. *I'm just tired and run down*, I thought again and again. When Mom or my friends asked if I was doing all right, I was always quick to respond, "I'm fine."

But even I was starting to wonder if that was really true.

One evening, as I was cleaning up after dinner, I bent down to pick up Skyler's sweater from the floor. When I stood back up, I felt a wave of dizziness wash over me, but moments later I was fine. So like every other symptom I was experiencing, I pushed this one away as well. Until it got to the point where I was getting dizzy every time I bent over. I would get a head rush and have to stand in place for a few moments, waiting for my head to clear so that I could go back to doing whatever I was doing.

Not only did I get head rushes, but I began turning purple in the face every time I bent over as well. It also happened whenever I would try to run or even just play the Nintendo Wii with Skye. I remember calling my mom while laughing as I was looking at myself in the mirror and thinking my shade of violet was absolutely hilarious. My reflection was astonishing, but not in a good way. I could not believe what I was seeing, so I joked that I looked just like Barney. My mother was not amused.

Back to the doctor I went. Once again, they were unable to find anything wrong with me. All of my levels were still within the normal ranges, and all my vitals were good.

I started to question myself, wondering if I was just imagining everything. Maybe I really did just need to get in better shape. Only the more I tried to exercise, the worse I felt.

By this time, I was starting to feel like I was losing my mind. Repeat trips back to my family doctor yielded the same results. I was being told there was nothing wrong with me and that there was no medical reason to explain the way I was feeling, even when doctors were reminded of my FM diagnosis. I suppose it didn't help that they knew nothing about FM and did not consider that to be a factor in any of my symptoms. They said the test results spoke for themselves. According to them, I was physically fine, which I desperately wanted to believe, but in the back of my mind was that voice whispering the truth.

I took Skyler to the mall with me one day, intent on doing a little shopping and having a fun girls day. Everything was going fine ... until it wasn't. Skyler and I were walking around, visiting our favorite stores, when I suddenly realized I had no idea where I was. I was just standing on the top floor of the mall, looking around but not recognizing anything. I didn't know where my car was or even why I was there. It was like there was a blank space in my mind, like there were moments when I felt completely and utterly lost.

Once I realized where I was, I called my mom. I was trying to laugh it off, telling her I had just experienced a "major brain fart," but her mother's intuition told her something was very wrong. She was extremely concerned and begged me to call the doctor right away. When I did, he advised me to go directly to the emergency room.

My mom said she would meet Skyler and me there. We arrived first, and I explained to the receptionist that I had fibrosing mediastinitis and was having terrible head rushes with chest pressure. Then I told her about my recent memory lapse and that my doctor had told me to come to the hospital for an evaluation. She looked at me and asked, "So you're here for a psych evaluation?"

I didn't even know what to say. I looked over at Skye, sitting in the chair next to me tracing her fingers over the armrest of the chair and pretending not to listen. In an instant, all the fear and anxiety I had suppressed over the years about this very moment came flooding back to me. I began crying and my heart was racing.

I worked with individuals with mental illnesses. Over the years, I had brought plenty of them to the emergency room for mental-health evaluations. And now, I was the one that was being questioned in regard to my mental stability. I just sat there with tears streaming down my face, thinking, *Please, God, let Mom get here before they commit me.*

I went through a battery of tests before being released with instructions to follow up with my doctor. Again, nothing was found. My oxygen levels were fine, my labs were okay, and everything looked normal.

Normal. Wasn't that what I had been striving for all along?

Still, I knew in my heart that nothing about this was normal. But I had been calling the doctor a lot, coming in for test after test, all to no avail. Finally, at yet another appointment, he sat me down and asked, "What is really going on?" He brought up the possibility of anxiety before offering me a prescription for Xanax.

My heart sank, and frustration took over.

I knew I had no other choice but to admit this was all related to FM. I knew myself. I knew I wasn't making it up, and I knew this wasn't anxiety. Instead, it was something so much worse. This meant I had to go back to my former specialists.

I ended up sitting in front of Dr. Wait once more, after years had passed since seeing him last. He ran more tests and finally showed me why I had been feeling the way I was. The results of my most recent CT scan showed that my superior vena cava (a vein that facilitates blood flow between the heart and upper half of the body) was 100 percent occluded. So I had an answer, but not much else. In fact, as he looked at the image, he said, "I can see why you feel like your head is going to explode. But I don't know how to help you."

He compared my head to a balloon filled to the brink with pressure and no way to release it. My diagnosis was now FM with superior vena cava syndrome—SVC syndrome for short. The scar tissue had obstructed my SVC, preventing blood flow from the upper part of my body to my heart. It explained everything: the terrible headaches, the chest pressure, turning purple, and even having periods of memory loss. It was all a result of such a limited blood flow to my head.

My body had developed collateral veins to compensate for my SVC being blocked off, but of course the veins were not sufficient enough. They were the same veins Dr. Wait had run into when performing my thoracotomy five years earlier. He explained now that it seemed as though the FM had most likely "died out," that the damage was done. That didn't mean I was cured; it just meant the disease had spread as far as it was going to. The damage that had already been done would eventually kill me. My body could only work at this level, overcompensating for what wasn't working, for so long. Now it was just a matter of waiting that out, accepting that the symptoms I was currently struggling with would probably continue to get worse over time.

It was bittersweet. Having my fears finally acknowledged and talking to a doctor who believed me was validating. But hearing once more that my fate was sealed was a hard pill to swallow. So I sat in that office and cried. Because finally I was being told by someone in the medical profession that I wasn't crazy.

While at the same time being reminded that I was dying.

Between my initial diagnosis and the point when I really started to experience symptoms, my insurance changed. My new insurance would no longer cover my trips to the Mayo Clinic, which became another barrier to treatment for me.

I felt as though I was starting this whole nightmare all over again. My disease was so rare, and I had come across very few doctors who knew anything at all about it. That hadn't been the case at the Mayo Clinic, and they already had all my records. But if I couldn't afford to see them, none of that really mattered.

I was extremely frustrated. At least the doctors at Mayo had heard of this disease. None of the local doctors I had seen or talked to knew anything about FM. But suddenly, it was my responsibility to find the needle-in-the-haystack doctor who understood my case. Then I would need to transfer my records over and do more testing, because no matter what testing had already been done, doctors always wanted to run their own. Once again, I found myself back at square one, with no choice but to dive in and get the process started. But I was frustrated and slightly bitter when it seemed like the closest referral was going to be waiting for me in Iowa City, Iowa.

In the meantime, I was so sick of being sick. I hated that I had no control over how I was feeling or what was happening to me. I felt awful all of the time now, to the point that I didn't even want to get out of bed. Nobody around me understood this disease or what I was experiencing, which made it even harder for me to talk about. I was almost embarrassed to tell anyone I had FM, afraid they would shoot me that look of panic and confusion I had grown so used to—the one that made it perfectly clear they were uncomfortable and didn't know how to respond.

I tried to downplay it all, both for myself and for them. "I mean so what? I have headaches. But everybody has headaches, right?" Only these headaches were so intense that I wanted to scream out in pain from even the slightest movements. At night, I had to sleep with my head elevated just to relieve the pressure.

The pressure in my chest was even worse, making it hard to breathe most days. I constantly felt like I was in the middle of getting a fierce bear hug, unable to expand my chest or escape the embrace of this disease. On top of that, I had this excruciating pain shooting through my back to my chest; it was a stabbing sensation that struck all the way through me like a knife being viciously pulled in and out, again and again.

I was absolutely miserable, but I learned it was easier to just tell everybody I was fine. At least that saved me the discomfort of having to explain FM to everyone I met. Plus how could I explain this disease to anyone when I myself was so confused about it? When even my doctors seemed to be at a loss? This disease was killing me, yet I couldn't find the words to tell anyone why or to explain what was causing it. It was all a jumble of explanations that never seemed to completely add up.

To make matters worse, I was young and in decent shape. So I *looked* completely healthy on the outside. Most of the people I met couldn't seem to comprehend how I could possibly be as sick as I said I was. I began to live in fear of being questioned, of being deemed a drama queen. I was afraid of those who might not believe me, who would look at me with skepticism and say, "But you don't look sick." So more often than not, I simply remained silent rather than opening the door to that inquisition.

Still, I *was* sick. Not just physically either. I was also sick of never-ending doctors' appointments. I was sick of feeling awful and nobody being able to do a thing for me. And I was sick of forever feeling like nobody understood. So I decided to go see my brother and his family.

My brother was finally out of the military, having moved Sarah and the kids to Wisconsin after completing his commission. My nieces Ashley and Emma were close to Skyler's age. The girls loved being together. Being with them was the perfect retreat when everything else started to seem too hard.

Shortly after I arrived, Ashley and Emma began jumping on the trampoline with Skye and playing the Wii. When I tried to join in, the girls asked me why I was purple. Sarah immediately jumped in, trying to reassure me by explaining that a lot of people turned red when trying to exercise or exert themselves. I had told myself the same, but looking in the mirror, I knew this wasn't that. My face looked like Veruca Salt in the midst of her blueberry transformation. I knew this was because my blocked SVC was once again reminding me that something was seriously wrong with me. And because other people were noticing the symptoms now as well, it made it harder to pretend that the writing wasn't all over the wall.

I really was dying.

That weekend went by too fast, and I was left alone with my thoughts once more on the drive back home. Skyler slept in the car as I began thinking about all that was going on in my life and how empty it had become. I had always been active. I loved doing anything outdoors—playing sports or just staying physical. But now I couldn't even bend over or walk a block without coughing and experiencing chest pains. Not to mention feeling like my head was going to explode or that I might pass out. Skyler had begun to notice the changes herself, and she often referred to me as having a "broken heart." The first time she said it, my heart actually did break.

On my bad days, which were becoming more and more frequent, I would tell her I was going to take a magic shower that would make me feel all better. As the warm water washed over me, I would cry out all of my frustrations, counting on the running water to mute the sound of my tears. Then I would come back out of the bathroom and assure her I was better, even though I wasn't. I convinced myself this was enough though. That for at least a few more years, she would continue to buy into the idea of the "magic shower."

I drove and reflected on all of this, only growing more and more furious at the turn my life had taken. By the time I dropped Skyler off at her dad's house, I was on the verge of breaking down. I drove only a few blocks away before I began crying uncontrollably, eventually needing to pull over. I just started screaming and hitting the steering wheel.

"God, why is this happening to me?" I yelled between sobs. "Wasn't the divorce enough? And diabetes? Haven't I been through enough?"

I hated being a part-time mom. I hated being alone. I just wanted to be normal and happy and to have something good happen in my life. I couldn't afford the ever-increasing pile of medical bills, all from doctors' appointments that did nothing to make me feel better. I felt like I would never find love again, because who would want a divorced mom who was already knocking on death's door? I was feeling so helpless. So alone. So sure that this was not the life I wanted to be living. And so completely lost in terms of how to change any of it.

During my drive, the only radio station that had come through was Christian. I had stopped at it purely to have something to listen to. But at that moment, rising just above the sound of my tears, a song came on about the rain being too heavy for your shoulders. The lyrics promised that God would be with you as you weathered the storm.

Looking back, that drive was a turning point for me. It was what some might call hitting rock bottom in terms of my grief, but it was also the moment when I was able to finally see that God was with me, that this was where my journey with Him would begin for this season of my life. That song felt like a message meant explicitly for me, timed perfectly to when I needed it most.

I continued listening to the lyrics, ever so slowly calming down as a result of their comfort. Eventually, I dried my eyes and felt infused by hope, suddenly curious about what Iowa City might bring.

Suddenly I was convinced that if I let Him, God would walk beside me and hold me up when I needed Him, no matter what lay ahead.

In July 2007, about four months after my symptoms started increasing in severity, I began to struggle with getting out of bed in the mornings. Some of that was depression, but a lot of it was also pure exhaustion. And pain. All the time pain. It was a fight every day just to force a smile across my face, and the only reason I even tried was to convince Skye that I was fine. That her mom hadn't left her yet.

Mom and Dad drove me to Iowa City when my appointment finally came around, but again, the news was not what we had hoped for. I heard the same line I had already heard so many times before: they were sorry, but this was a horrible disease and there was no cure for it.

There was no hope. Not even a single word to encourage us.

It was during that visit that I brought up the ten-year prognosis I had been given in 2002. I joked, "I've had this disease for five years, so only five years to go, right?" The doctor didn't smile back. So instead, I simply asked, "Am I really dying?"

I don't know what I expected her to say, but the look on her face gave me my answer. She finally nodded her head and said, "Yes." She explained that the prognosis was not good, and then she advised me to start making arrangements for Skyler.

It was all I could to keep myself upright in this moment.

She went on to explain that with this disease, the focus should be on "the quality of life, not the quantity of life." It was a phrase that would haunt me for years to come. I was in disbelief, looking at my parents for some sort of reassurance that this woman was wrong, that I would be just fine. But for a split second, I saw the truth in their eyes. My parents were not able to tell me everything was going to be okay. Their mouths hung open as they just stared at the doctor, as shocked and scared as I was. But then a flush of red overtook my mother's face. She took on a tone of authority, explaining that we would not be leaving this hospital until we spoke to someone who had better news. Or at least some sort of plan.

I always thought my mom was a little too vocal, and there were times in the past when this had embarrassed me. But right now, this was not one of those times. I was grateful she was there to speak with the strength I wasn't sure I possessed.

She demanded we see someone else, and the doctor complied. But as we went from doctor to doctor, visiting nearly every department in the hospital, we just kept hearing the same thing.

There was no hope. No answers. I should start planning for the end.

Feeling defeated, I sat in yet another room at yet another patient table waiting for yet another doctor to come in and talk to us. I finally stood, the tears breaking free from my eyes, and I told my mom I just wanted to go home. But she refused to leave, even blocking the door so I could not walk out. She seemed convinced that if we just kept pushing, we would find someone who could help.

Unfortunately, the next doctor had nothing to offer us either.

Before heading back home, we all went to the bathroom to regroup. It was there that we each sobbed in the stalls, a pathetic attempt at not crying in front of each other.

I thought, *What am I supposed to be learning from this, God? What is the purpose?*

My frustration had turned to defeat, and for the first time, it hit me. This disease was *not* a better alternative to cancer.

I felt horrible all the time. I was dying, and nobody could help. This time, doctors didn't even suggest any of the three treatment options that had been offered before. They simply told me there was no cure, that there was nothing they could do for me. I even brought up the use of chemotherapy but was told that as a treatment option, that had fizzled due to the lack of success.

Again, all the doctors could tell me was that this was a horrible disease. But everyone I spoke to lacked information on treatments that had yielded any sort of success, while simultaneously being unable to tell me how many people had really died from this disease. They simply knew nothing. I looked normal and healthy, so every time I mentioned FM and my symptoms, even the doctors would look at me like I was crazy. I was tired of hearing, "But you don't look sick." Did I need to be hooked up to oxygen, be bald, or be unable to walk before people would take me seriously?

Once we finally got home, I sat in a corner with a dim lamp on and just stared at the wall. The scrapbook I had made for Skyler caught my attention. I took it over to the couch and sat quietly, looking through the pictures that I had carefully arranged for her.

She loved looking through this scrapbook and always laughed at one picture of herself in particular. She was three years old, sitting in running pants without a shirt on, covered in ink after a rebellious few minutes spent drawing all over herself.

"Were you mad?" she would always ask between fits of laughter.

I again began crying, fearful this scrapbook would be the only thing my daughter would remember me by. I sat there thinking about how much of a battle it was just to get out of bed in the morning and perform simple daily tasks. I couldn't even bend over to switch the laundry or pick up a pair of socks anymore. At least, not without getting a head rush and turning purple. I was always in so much physical pain, and I was mentally exhausted. I wasn't even making fun memories with her anymore. I was just her sick mom.

I began to focus on all of the bad in my life, dwelling on my mistakes. In the past, I would spend the weeks that I didn't have Skyler putting on my headphones and going for runs around the neighborhood. I loved getting lost in the music and feeling the burn from a good workout. But that was no more. Since I was now no longer able to spend my time doing the things I loved doing outdoors, I found myself socializing and having drinks with my friends at the local bars more and more often. And when I was drinking, I often made choices I regretted. I wasn't living the life I wanted to be living, but maybe that was at least partially because I wasn't able to live the life I wanted to live anymore.

I tried to embrace that feeling I had experienced when sitting in my car after the last visit with my brother, listening to a song that reminded me that God was by my side. But I realized I was not living with God in the driver's seat. Honestly, he was nowhere near my car. I knew that was at least partially my fault.

I even began to feel like God was punishing me for the divorce and for me putting Skyler through such a horrible situation. I had asked for forgiveness before, pleaded for it, but what if that wasn't enough?

God, what else do You want?

I put the scrapbook down and went to bed, only to cry myself to sleep yet another night.

Mom and Dad saw me struggling physically as well as emotionally. They tried to talk to me about my faith, hoping that finding God again might at least give me the strength to get through this. At times, I wanted to follow them. But other times, I resisted. Perhaps because I was stubborn. And angry.

I grew up with great parents who prayed, took us to church, had family devotions, and set the example of how a godly family should be. Yet I had always struggled, off and on, with my faith. The first time I stopped going to church was right after I got married. Skyler's dad had doubts about God. And with so many of the questions that he had, I too started to wonder if there really was a God. Plus I had simply become too busy to put any effort into my relationship with God. I wasn't even reading the Bible during that time. At first, it seemed fine—normal, even. But over time, I started to feel guilty. I was sorry that I did not know Him as well as I knew He wanted me to. I had been saved, but I knew I was not acting like I was a believer or a follower of Christ.

I came back to the church when we separated, but then I got sick. It had been harder to stay strong in my faith than ever before. How could I worship a God who would allow me to be taken from my daughter?

I was watching *Evan Almighty* with my parents one night, and at one point, the main character said, "I know, I know. Whatever you do, you do because you love me. Do me a favor? Love me less?"

The movie itself really hit me pretty hard. I found myself wondering how God could have so completely turned his back on me if He really did love me. How could He have allowed this to happen? Was it because He loved me so much that I was feeling so adrift right now? If that was the case, I agreed with Evan Baxter; I wanted Him to love me a little less.

I had been praying and praying for God to let this end, to heal me. And while I was still in denial that the outcome I had been told over and over again was an inevitability, I continued praying for the doctors to be able to do *something* to help me feel better. Something to "fix" me. Even just that morning, I had been praying for strength so that Skyler and my family would not see how weak I really was. And then, perhaps when I needed it most, there was another line in the movie that seemed to speak to everything I was feeling.

It went something like this:

> Let me ask you something. If someone prays for patience, do you think God gives them patience? Or does He give them the opportunity to be patient? If someone prays for courage, does God give them courage, or does He give them opportunities to be courageous? If someone prays for a closer relationship, do you think God zaps them with warm, fuzzy feelings, or does He give them the opportunities to love each other?

At this point, the tears were streaming down my face. After that line, I really started to understand how God might be working with me in this. And after the movie, I told my parents that I was truly going to start reevaluating how I prayed.

From the beginning, they had been telling me God knew what He was doing and everything would be okay. But I hadn't believed them. I even grew frustrated with them on occasion, wanting to yell, "*How can you say God knows what He's doing? How is everything going to be okay when even the doctors don't know how to help me? If God wanted to cure me, He could easily show Himself to me and take away all of the pain that I am going through.*" I thought it was that simple. Or at least that it should be. And the fact that it wasn't had me feeling abandoned on more than one occasion. But my parents had the strength and faith that I was lacking. They believed, even when I knew this situation was killing them inside.

I wanted so badly to have the same faith.

I tried to stay busy, still hoping to distract myself from the reality I was living. My mom was always there, desperate to spend time with me, her love forever radiating through. She agreed to do almost anything I suggested, even going to see *Blades of Glory* with me one afternoon. The movie was terrible, and at first, I was laughing that she was even there with me at all—proof that she would do anything to spend time with me. But then I was hit by this awful fear that if my mom would go see even this movie with me, I really must be dying. For a moment, complete panic overtook me. But then I burst out laughing at the ridiculousness of this thought. Of course, I was dying. Countless doctors had already confirmed this. So why would it take my mom watching this stupid movie with me for that thought to finally settle in?

As morbid as it was, and as terrible as the movie was, that one thought actually gave us something to laugh about together—something we both desperately needed.

I went home that afternoon and began looking at the FM support group again, determined to at least do something proactive. For weeks, I mostly just read along, never commenting or joining in on the conversations myself. There was something strangely comforting now about knowing at least I wasn't alone in this. There were so many people struggling, in so much physical and mental anguish, and nobody could help them. When I had first stumbled upon this site, I felt so distant from everyone there. But now their stories were strikingly just like mine.

Tricia's story, in particular, stood out to me, perhaps because our stories were so similar. She was a young mother and had the same symptoms I had been experiencing, except her symptoms had improved with stents in both her SVC and pulmonary artery.

It was something. A treatment I hadn't yet been offered. A possibility of hope?

I rarely talked about my disease, or about the looming deadline attached to my death. When I did talk about it, I made jokes, unable to embrace the seriousness of what was happening around others. But in the back of my mind, I always knew what I was up against. I was always fully aware of how my body was betraying me. And sometimes, in the deepest, darkest recesses of my mind, I would begin to wish that FM would just do its job and take me away, that it would put an end to all this suffering, anguish, and fear. I sometimes convinced myself that because I had Skyler only every other week, she was used to me not being there for her anyway. There were times when I wished my parents would just let me be and leave all this alone. If nobody could help me, why did they keep insisting that we go back to Iowa City?

In truth, I had slowly been giving up. But there was one more appointment in the books in Iowa City, and while reading the pages of that support group, I started to compile my own list of possibilities—things that had provided at least some relief for others. I began arming myself with information.

And then I heard there was one person who *might* be able to help me.

My appointment wasn't with Dr. Youness. In fact, he was hesitant to talk with us; it was his day off, and he wasn't in his white gown. He had stopped by the hospital to pick something up, not planning to see any patients at all. But he knew what FM was, and my parents and I now knew about him. So my mom took over, insisting that we talk to him. She claimed we would not leave until we did.

Looking back, I wonder how my parents and I were not arrested or banned from the hospital for our display of stubbornness.

Within a few minutes of talking with Dr. Youness, I felt hope. Not only did he know what FM was, but he also said he could put stents in my SVC via angioplasty and ballooning, which would greatly improve my symptoms. He explained that this was one treatment option that had not been offered years back but that he had success stories of others who had received stents due to conditions like mine.

At first, even knowing what I had already read online, it was hard to believe this could be that easy. I mean he had to be joking with us, right? We had been to Mayo over and over again ... and nothing. Then we had visited every doctor in every department here at Iowa City, all to no avail. But now this guy was acting like the solution was no big deal?

Surely, it was too good to be true. But we didn't care. It was *something*. Of course, I was going to do it!

I was scheduled to have the procedure done a few days later. My parents were ecstatic and praised God as I fought the voice in my head telling me this couldn't possibly be so easy.

The day of the procedure, my parents took me to their church and asked the other worshippers to pray for me. Many of the people, including my parents, laid their hands on me and said a prayer. We were all crying.

I had slowly been reaching out more and more to God, trying to trust and believe that He would get me through this. But I still struggled a lot and experienced moments of wanting to throw in the towel. Over the last several months, I had cried and yelled at God more than I cared to admit. But I had also tried to make sure and thank Him for carrying me through. My faith was slowly getting stronger, and I was finally starting to feel somewhat good about my upcoming procedure.

My sister Michelle surprised me and showed up at the hospital for my surgery. She had taken the day off from work to be there. I was anxious, excited, and nervous about what was to come. But most of all, I was hungry—complaining to my entire family that the whole presurgery fasting thing was not my favorite. Michelle, my sincere and sympathetic older sister, ate a candy bar over my bed so that it would crumble in front of me onto the sheet. Her sense of humor really helped ease my fears, and her presence did take my mind off things. At least for a little bit.

I was shown to the bathroom, where I had to remove my jeans and top and put on a gown before being sent back to bed. The nurses explained that the doctor would be accessing both of my upper arms; therefore I had a PICC line in each arm, and one in my hand for meds.

Finally, it was time. My parents said another prayer, we hugged and said our I-love-yous, and then I was rolled away in the bed. The last look I saw on my parents' faces was a mixture of worry and hope.

I met a team of great nurses and doctors back in the operating room. They began by having me move to a long, thin table where I lay flat on my back. They then slid two hard boards underneath me, so that I could stretch my arms out like I was flying. The medical staff was awesome and made a few different comments that made me laugh, which helped me to feel somewhat at ease. They continued to joke throughout their explanations, giving each other a hard time as well and engaging in small talk with me. It was all hugely beneficial in keeping my mind from wandering back to all of the what-ifs.

Of course, I also heard a lot of "But you're so young" and "You don't look sick." That was par for the course by this point.

The room was cold, but not as cold as the bright-orange dye that they saturated my arms in for sterilization. Dr. Youness would be making a small incision in each of my upper arms for the procedure, so it was necessary to make sure the entire area was clean.

Shortly after that, they brought a blue tarplike material and created a tent over my face. I began to get anxious as the reality started to sink in.

What if this doesn't work? What if something happens and I die? What if I can't be there for Skyler? What if, what if, what if ...

And then the medicine kicked in. I was relaxed but never fully asleep. I had to stay awake for the procedure, which was a whole new level of bizarre. Dr. Youness explained everything they were doing as it happened, but all I could focus on was what felt like a worm traveling through my arms.

All of a sudden, I felt a tremendous pressure in the middle of my back. I began to tear up, thinking the medications were obviously not working. I would later find out that this was where the blockage had been and that Dr. Youness was able to break through.

Four hours later, I will never forget the excitement and smiles splashed across my family's faces as they told me Dr. Youness had successfully put four stents in my SVC. I had blood flow again!

They said the before and after results of the scan were miraculous. Michelle reported that in the first scan, before my surgery, she really didn't know what she should be looking for. It wasn't until Dr. Youness opened my SVC with four stents and the after images were presented that Michelle saw how bad my blood flow really had been. She said she "finally got it" and was able to see why I had been feeling the way I had been feeling for so long.

We knew at that moment that God had brought Dr. Youness into my life. His role had been to give me another chance.

My family and I felt instantly indebted to Dr. Youness, knowing that from the day we had met him, he had been confident about helping me. And he followed through.

I went home that same night amazed that the chest pressure, the headaches, the head rushes, and turning purple had all disappeared. Even my eyesight seemed to be clearer. I hadn't thought my vision had been affected until the drive home, when I realized all the colors in front of me looked so much crisper and clearer than they had in a very long time.

I immediately got back on the FM support group and updated my story, excited to tell them I could now bend over and pick up Skyler's socks from the floor without getting a head rush or turning purple. So many people congratulated me, but it was also hard to recognize how many of them had not experienced the same fortunate outcome I had. For many, stents weren't even an option because their disease had progressed too far. I was one of the very few fortunate ones for whom this could work.

I realized that for a lot of those struggling, the beauty of the support group was that it connected them with others who were experiencing the same lows they were. This disease left you feeling so isolated and alone; there was something nice about being able to connect with those who truly understood. Those who could relate and were experiencing something similar.

For those of us who were doing well though? We didn't need the support so much. And just as a doctor had once told me, the focus of this disease needed to be on quality of life, not quantity. Those struggling didn't really want to be confronted by those who were currently doing well, and those doing well didn't want to be brought down by the reminders of how this disease could still affect them in the future.

In a sense, life was literally too short to dwell on the bad when we were in the middle of the good.

I started pulling away from the group. Not because I didn't want to support others but because I wanted to enjoy this healthy period while I had it. I also didn't want to be the reason any of those currently struggling ever felt like their safe place was no longer the place they could go to feel safe and welcomed by those currently walking a similar path.

I recognized the group for what it was, knowing it would always be there for me if I needed it. But I was grateful that, for the time being, I was feeling healthy enough to walk away.

In the meantime, I also did an article for our local newspaper on fibrosing mediastinitis since the last several years, especially the last several months, had been so emotional and heart wrenching because of this disease that nobody knew anything about. I did the article with a desire to bring awareness of FM through what I had experienced, but unfortunately, there were no references to the web sites I had directed the reporter to attach.

Ten days later, it felt like my entire world had been turned around. I was so excited and thankful to be feeling better that I went out with my friends to celebrate. We went to a local sports bar where music was playing and I was dancing, double-checking again and again with my friends that I wasn't turning purple. They would just laugh and reassure me that no, I was not purple. It all felt like such dream.

I was just so happy. Not partying in the sad, desperate way I had been over the previous few years—looking for ways to numb my pain—but simply enjoying the night for what it was. I was laughing, smiling, and genuinely feeling optimistic about what was to come.

Making this the perfect moment for God to put His next surprise directly in my path.

My friends and I were talking when I looked across the room and noticed a man sitting with a friend of his own. I did a double take, immediately attracted to what I could see of him in the inconspicuous looks I was stealing. He had short, dark-brown hair with this little messed-up flip in the front, and he was wearing a blue-and-white striped, long-sleeve shirt with a white T-shirt peeking out from underneath.

It seemed like every time I glanced in his direction, he was already looking at me. And then, sure enough, he and his friend came over and introduced themselves.

His name was Tim. We made some small talk, but my friends were ready to go. After a quick trip to the bathroom, I didn't have a chance to say good-bye before being whisked out the door. I thought about him throughout the night, and well into the next day, so I finally convinced a friend of mine to go back to the sports bar with me. And sure enough, there he was.

Tim and his friend came over yet again, asking us to play a game of pool. Some of my friends from work had shown up as well, so we were all just hanging out in a big group. I was filling one of my coworkers in on my recent surgery and we were both crying. She was just so happy that I was finally feeling better. Then I whispered to her about Tim, and she confirmed that he was, indeed, very cute.

Eventually, he asked me to join him for a drink. We went to a table and started talking. His first question, of course, was if I was married. As much as I hated to admit it, I told him that I was divorced and not seeing anybody. Having been brought up in a Christian home, with parents who had been together my entire life, I always felt a bit of shame in discussing my divorce. It had been such a difficult time. But there it was now, out in the open.

His next question was whether or not I had any kids. I replied by telling him about Skyler, who was still seven (but going on sixteen). It felt good to talk about her and to have everything out in the open. It had been so long since I had dated, I wasn't even sure how to have these conversations anymore. But I figured he could either take it or leave it. Although I hoped he would still be interested.

He then shared with me that he had a three-year-old son, and I learned that he lived just a couple of blocks away from me. Skyler and I had actually walked by his house on several occasions.

He talked about how he drove a Harley and was rebuilding a Camaro. The football game was on in the background, and he revealed that he was a Green Bay Packers fan. A diehard Minnesota Vikings fan myself, I joked that we could no longer be friends.

We continued to make small talk, but every once in a while, my coworker would pop in and tell Tim what a great person I was, that I was just so sweet and he would be stupid to pass me up. Then she said he should ask me out, and I was sure I must be turning every shade of purple again. But Tim looked at her, grinned, and finally said, "Well, that's what I'm trying to do, if you would just give me a chance." She smiled at me, I gave Tim my number, and then my friends and I left.

I waited patiently for him to call, even telling my mom that I thought this was a guy I might be able to really like, which of course made me feel he probably wouldn't call, because surely I couldn't be that lucky. My biggest concern was that the local newspaper had just done an article about me, my FM, and how rare my disease was, hoping to bring awareness to the condition. At the time, it had been an opportunity I was really excited about. But now I was afraid he would see that, think I was off my rocker, and lose my number. But a few days later, I received yet another phone call that would forever change my life.

This time, for the better.

My stomach did flip-flops as Tim and I spoke. He was in the middle of making dinner for his son Nathan, and there were a lot of awkward silences. But still, I was excited just to be talking to him.

He asked me if I would like to go out to dinner with him, and I said I would love that, but I joked that I tended to be pretty quiet so it would be up to him to keep the conversation going. That was only followed by more silence on his part—the first indication that Tim was pretty quiet himself. I smiled a little, thinking that this date could really go either way.

We agreed that since I already knew where he lived I would just meet him at his house. Truthfully, that felt safer to me than giving him my address. I still didn't really know this man. But just like that, our first date was planned.

I was a nervous wreck, feeling like I was back in high school again. It had been so long since I had been on an actual date. Between the divorce, being sick, taking care of Skyler, and working seven days a week when she wasn't with me, there hadn't been much time for dating. It had never felt like a priority. But now, with Tim, there was something that I felt drawn to. He would later argue it was his good looks and rippling biceps, but I knew it was more than that. Even then, so early on, there was just something there.

As I pulled up in front of his house that night, getting out and walking up to the door, Tim came out to greet me, and my heart stopped. It had been about two weeks since we had last seen each other, parenting commitments on both ends getting in the way of making a date earlier, and I had forgotten how handsome he was. He was wearing jeans with a red T-shirt. He flashed that smile of his that took my breath away, in a good way and not in a scary FM way. But then we got in the car, him driving, and an awkward silence set in.

I joked, reminding him that he had agreed to break the silence and keep the conversation going if this should happen. So he jumped right in and tried, mostly with small talk, but ... it was something.

We got to dinner, and as the awkwardness dissipated, he opened up to me and explained he would soon be moving in with his brother, due to some medical issues he was dealing with. I would later find out that he was actually moving in with his parents, but he didn't want to tell me that on our first date. If only he had known that I had lived with my own parents for a short period following my divorce, there was nothing to be embarrassed about as far as I was concerned.

I wanted to ask about what he was dealing with medically, but that felt too invasive for a first date. And I wasn't feeling totally ready to open up to him about FM either. So instead, I allowed the topic to pass, assuming he would tell me more when he felt comfortable.

We had a great first date, talking mostly about our families and our interests. All of the typical stuff. I had ordered a cheeseburger, solely because I was craving the pickles I knew would be served with it. As Tim and I got to know each other, I laughed upon finding out that he absolutely hated pickles. He couldn't even stand to have them anywhere near his food, let alone on his plate. And there I was, on our first date, shoving them in my mouth like they were the most delicious things I had ever tasted.

Classic.

I had been on my own for so long now that the idea of letting a man pay for my meal felt uncomfortable. Call it an independent streak if you will, but I insisted on picking up the bill. And he let me. So looking back, I guess it kind of serves him right that he had to put up with my pickle infatuation!

After dinner, we drove back to his house. He invited me inside, and as soon as I walked in, I was a bit surprised by how sparsely decorated it was. There was simply an entertainment center with a TV and some movies, a couch and a futon, and a kitchen table and chairs. I started to wonder if he really had a son, because there were no pictures or toys anywhere to be seen. Not even a kids movie. But just as alarm bells started going off for me, he reminded me he would be moving very soon and that he had most of their stuff packed up. The house had already been sold, so it made sense there wasn't much left.

We watched a movie and he remained a perfect gentleman the entire time. When it was over, he walked me to the door and gave me a very sweet kiss. I thanked him for the nice time and walked out feeling as light as air. It had been a great first date, and I was surprised that I hadn't been more nervous than I was. I had actually talked and made conversation. It was all just so … normal.

A few days later, Skyler and I were outside playing basketball, and sure enough, there was Tim sitting in his car at the stop sign across the street. He was just passing by when he looked over my way. We stared at each other the whole time with him realizing this was my apartment and me thinking, *Great. Now this guy knows where I live.*

It wasn't like it was the end of the world. I liked him, and he had given me no reason not to trust him. But I was just so new to dating.

We talked a few days later, and he explained that he had been coming home from the bank when he spotted me. The next day, he showed up on my doorstep with some purple mums, explaining that they were all he could afford, but that he had wanted to bring me flowers. My heart melted a little. To this day, mums are still my favorite.

After a few more phone calls and dates, Tim finally confessed to me that he was actually moving in with his parents, and I shared with him that I had once needed to do the same. He told me that his brother and one of his sisters, as well as their families, all lived within ten to fifteen minutes of their parents' house and that the entire family was close. Tim was the baby, the youngest of four.

With his house sold, there was last-minute cleaning and fixing up to be done. Of course, I offered to help. In reality, my role was more to keep him company as he did what he needed to do. We ran to Lowe's one afternoon. I watched him picking out what he needed, with him looking the picture of perfection to me in his baseball hat and green muscle shirt with the sleeves ripped off. His arms were amazing. I laughed and thought, *You have got to be kidding me,* because I thought for sure he was flexing on purpose. But no, his arms just looked that good. I felt myself go all mushy inside.

Everything about this man was making me smile, and we had just met. Still, these butterflies I was feeling were undeniable.

Everything was going great.

We had only been on a few dates, but it was very clear that something real was happening between us. I liked him. A *lot*. And I knew that he felt the same about me; however, this was a time when neither Tim nor I had God as our main focus in life.

We always managed to end up at the bars with the usual crowd, which only led to long nights of drinking. This was not contributing anything to the growth of our relationship. Instead, it became an annoying habit for me.

It was then that I opened my eyes and took a long, hard look at the way I was living my life. It wasn't as though I was some horrible person. I was a good mom, a good friend, a good employee, and a good daughter. Even the ways in which I struggled were justifiable. I don't think anyone would have argued that I didn't have a right to be angry or sad. A lot had gone on in my life over the last few years, and I had been swallowing most of it down—pretending that I was fine when I was anything but.

Still, I had been making some choices that weren't reflective of the person I wanted to be. And I realized that I needed to stop hanging out with some of the people that I was spending my time with. Not because they were bad people but because

I was finding myself in situations that I really did not want to be a part of. And when I was with them, I wasn't being true to myself.

I had experienced these same thoughts so many times before, but something about meeting and getting to know Tim gave me a glimpse of all that was still available to me. I wanted so much more than the life I was living. I wanted so much more for Skyler—and for myself.

While Tim and I had just met, there was something about him that I did not want to risk losing. I really felt like we had the possibility of something great together. I started to pull away from certain friends. I wanted to prove to Tim, and myself, that I was so much better than how I had been acting. I had gotten into a vicious cycle, and because of Tim, I also started to realize how much I had strayed from God.

Tim helped me to regain focus in my life and to remember what really matters. I like to think I was able to do the same for him.

While at my sickest, I gained a true appreciation for so much that I had previously taken for granted. One of those things was simply being strong enough and healthy enough to run. So shortly after I got my stents in, I started doing just that: running.

A few months later, I competed in my first 5k. My dad and nephew Tyler ran with me. As we crossed the finish line, my eyes spilled over with tears and I was filled with so much gratitude. Just months before, this accomplishment would have been an impossibility. There had been no hope, and I had been far too sick to run even down the street, let alone for an entire race. I couldn't wipe the smile from my face now, even as the tears continued to fall.

My mom, of course, told anyone and everyone who would listen just how amazing this was for me, as she too succumbed to the tears. My dad put his arm around me and gave me the tightest of squeezes, indicating how proud he was as well. I felt so happy in this moment. So blessed to be exactly where I was.

Tim and I continued to see each other, and even though he had moved in with his parents, he spent a lot of time at my apartment during the weeks when Skyler wasn't with me. His family lived on a farm, so he was also helping out there as well. One of our dates consisted of meeting him over in the field to ride in the combine. I had grown up in Cedar Falls and was a city girl at heart, so riding in a tractor sounded like fun. Little did I know that I would one day wind up owning one of my own.

I had finally shared with Tim the history of my disease and how it had been such an ordeal over the last several years. I timidly admitted that I had originally been given ten years to live while also explaining that the doctors at that time knew very little about my illness. I shared with him the fact that only weeks before I met him I had found a doctor who actually disagreed with all of the other doctors. That doctor said that I would be around for a long time. That I would be able to live my life. I told Tim that this doctor had put in stents that now had me feeling the best I'd felt since being diagnosed.

My impression at the time was that I was cured, so I told Tim I was "good to go." I even drove this point home by telling him that another doctor had told me my FM had died out, that whatever symptoms I had now would be the only thing I had to worry about. And with the stents, I had no symptoms at all! The damage I had experienced from the disease had been "fixed." And being symptom free, in my mind, made me feel like I had conquered this disease. So that was what I told Tim.

Around the same time, he opened up to me about a surgery he had coming up. He explained that he had had a double-hernia procedure done a few years before we met but his body had rejected the mesh; therefore, the extreme pain in his stomach and groin continued to prevent him from lifting Nathan and playing with him the way that he truly wanted to. It hurt him to run, it hurt him if he was roughhousing with the kids, and it hurt him whenever anything had even a slight impact with his stomach.

Tim had tried so many options to relieve his pain, but nothing worked. He went from doctor to doctor at the major hospitals, even at the Mayo Clinic and Iowa City hospitals, trying to get them to remove the mesh. But due to the scar tissue and the mesh being such a twisted mess, most doctors refused to touch him. Except for one in Omaha who was willing to try surgery. This doctor was confident that he could at least remove some of the mesh to give Tim some relief. Tim would never be back to 100 percent, but the doctor was hopeful that he could at least make some difference.

As Tim shared his story with me, I couldn't believe the similarities we had in trying to find a doctor to help us with our rare obstacles. We began to joke saying our bodies were "meshed" for each other, as we both had scar tissue that was causing too many problems for us.

When it came time for his surgery, I was there with him, waiting and supporting alongside his parents. As much as I had wanted to be there, it was hard not to feel uncomfortable. I had been dating Tim for a few months and had only briefly met his parents in passing, yet there I was trying to make small talk with them while their son was in surgery. It felt awkward, to say the least.

That surgery turned into a seven-hour procedure, and our small talk quickly dried up. They were very nice to me though. There was even a point when the doctor came in to describe what they were dealing with, and he mentioned there was one potential problem that could prevent Tim from having kids in the future. The doctor explained that he would continue to do the best that he could with repairing and reconstructing Tim's stomach as well as the surrounding areas in order to give him the best outcome for a more rewarding future.

My own parents had started to express concern that I was spending so much time with someone I had just met. They seemed even more worried when I joined him for this surgery in Omaha. But I knew what it was like to have pain and to be struggling with health issues no one seemed able to fix. I also knew what it meant to have one doctor say that he could help. I wanted to be there for him for that, because I knew personally how important this surgery was to him.

After we returned home from his surgery, I realized that I was falling in love with Tim. As our six-month anniversary rolled around, we both agreed it was time for us to meet each other's kids.

Nathan was three at the time. Tim brought him over wearing a little John Deere hat, which he was just precious in. Nathan was very quiet, but I was able to get a few smiles out of him. Of course, Tim made Skyler laugh immediately. He put her at ease so quickly, and I knew in that moment that God had truly blessed me with a wonderful man.

Tim was recovering from his surgery, though his stomach continued to have some soreness because the doctor had not been able to remove all of the mesh. Tim was able to move around more and laugh without pain, yet he still had to be very careful with things he lifted and certain movements that he made.

From there, we started living our lives almost like a family, including the kids in a lot of our adventures. We went camping together, Tim and Nathan in one tent and Skyler and me in the other, which the kids absolutely loved. We went fishing and played ball, took bike rides, and swam at the beach. We were having so much fun.

One camping trip took a scary turn when we ended up in the middle of a tornado warning. The wind started picking up, so we loaded the kids in the car and packed up as quickly as we could. Shortly thereafter, a tree crashed down behind us in the other campsite. Before driving off, Tim said a quick prayer for God to keep us safe. It caught me off guard, as this was the first time he had prayed openly in front of me. Actually, with the exception of my dad, this was the first time any man had ever prayed in front of me.

I realized I really liked it; there was something comforting about his open display of faith. This led Tim and me to become open about our faith with each other. We both shared how we had drifted away from the church and reading the Bible but wanted to rebuild that relationship with God. The fact that we both wanted it helped us to encourage each other to work on our own personal relationships with God. Tim told me that it was because of me that he wanted to become a better man. It was absolutely corny, but I loved it. It was also because of him that I wanted to be a better woman.

Shortly after that, Tim invited me to attend church with him. We began going just about every Sunday, whether we had the kids or not. Having seen the role God played in my parents' marriage, and how not having faith at the center of my own marriage had worked to destroy it, sharing this with Tim now felt important. It felt right. I was sitting in church with Tim's arm around me one day, and I felt like life could not get any better than this. After so many tough years behind me, things were finally looking up.

I was feeling healthy and enjoying the life my stents had given me, living like I had no health concerns and jumping at every opportunity presented to me. In 2008, I went on a canoe trip to the Boundary Waters (a gorgeous wilderness region straddling the Canada/United States border) with my dad, sister, and her family. They had been there before, but this would be my first trip. I was excited and scared at the same time.

Knowing we would be portaging through the woods, we loaded up the canoes and packed our food and bags as lightly as possible. We were going to be carrying all of our belongings, along with our canoes, through the dry land to get from lake to lake, and I was ecstatic. I was given the rundown on all the "rules" for a safe and fun trip, the most important advice from my sister being to sing, clap, and make a lot of noise whenever I was going to the bathroom. She explained that making a spectacle of myself would scare off any bears that might be lurking.

I fell in love with the Boundary Waters that trip. Dad had been there several times before and was able to pick some of the easier portages to do, designing our trip around my novice abilities. Everyone still kind of babied me, not only because it was my first time portaging but also because of my medical history; they didn't want me overdoing anything. But I was confident in my abilities and just happy to be there.

The weather was gorgeous and the views were breathtaking. One morning, as my dad and I were exploring, we paddled around a set of rocks and came upon a huge bald eagle. I had never been so close to one before, and we both sat there in quiet amazement.

By the end of the trip, I had some scratches and bruises, but I wore them like badges of honor. This was why I had gotten the stents in the first place: to be active and experience life again.

Everything was falling into place. I was happy. I was healthy. I was in love. And I could feel God's presence in all of it.

After just under one year of dating, Tim was offered a job managing a hog building in 2008. Knowing his new responsibilities would require him to go to the building at least twice a day, every day, we decided to take a vacation by ourselves before he started.

Since we shared a love for the outdoors, I had bragged to him profusely about my experience portaging through the

Boundary Waters. Tim joked that everything about it sounded perfect, minus the portaging.

We did some research and he found a place near Crescent Lake in Minnesota, where we could camp out and be near the Boundary Waters, without the portaging. We were able to take his parents' boat. We caught some huge fish and had an amazing time. The days were warm, and the nights were cool, creating the perfect setting for some romantic campfires. Everything was peaceful and calm.

We took the boat out one night in particular and had a blast. Tim did a little bit of fishing until the sun got too low in the sky, and then we just cruised along the lake while enjoying the scenery. The sunset was beautiful, casting this fiery red color across the water, intermixed with yellow and orange tones. It was like something straight out of a movie.

When we got back to the campground, I couldn't find my lounge pants, which I wanted so that I could get comfortable out by the fire. I went into the tent to look for them, came back out, and then went back in. I was getting frustrated, searching everywhere and coming up empty-handed. Tim seemed a little anxious as well, but I just assumed it was my frustration rubbing off on him. But finally, he stopped me in front of the tent, put his arms around me, and then guided my head down with his hands, imploring me to look at the ground. There in the rocks he had spelled out, "Will you marry me?" I was stunned and excited. Fighting back the tears, I said, "Yes."

Tim and I returned from our trip and shared the news with Skyler and Nathan. They got along great, so they were very happy that they would have a consistent play buddy around.

Tim and I opted for a winter wedding, as we wanted our special day to be out of the ordinary. We planned a wedding within a six-month time frame and got married in January 2009. Skyler and Nathan were the little bride and groom, and they loved walking down the aisle. Or, I should say, Skyler kind of pulled Nathan down the aisle.

Everything went perfectly. Even better, Tim had a surprise honeymoon planned and had me opening gifts for hints every hour until we reached our destination. The final gift I opened was a snow angel on skis. We pulled up to Cascade Mountain at Wisconsin Dells, a gorgeous winter setting that provided the perfect backdrop for our honeymoon.

I couldn't have asked for more. Tim and I were getting our focus back on God; we were in love. I was 100 percent confident that this was the man God had intended for me to share my life with.

Shortly before we were married, Tim bought a three-bedroom farmhouse outside of Sumner, mainly for the calf nursery that was on the land. The house was a disaster and the property had been foreclosed, but he had dreams of raising cattle.

I remember walking into the house and thinking I would catch another disease, as it had this terribly strong pet odor and was beyond dirty. I entered the kitchen first, noticing the nice white cupboards that were covered in black dirt. Just off the kitchen was an extremely small bathroom and bedroom. As I walked into the dining-slash-living room, I noticed that the walls were yellow and the carpet was brown. Everything smelled awful and was stained.

Up the stairs were a small hallway and two decent-sized bedrooms that would eventually become Skyler's and Nathan's rooms. But right now, it was all a mess—to the extent that I really had a hard time imagining our family ever living here.

Tim took me back down through the kitchen and to another set of stairs that led to the basement. There we found beer cans in the rafters and a smell that was musty from water stains on the floor and walls.

I wasn't sure what Tim had been thinking, but from the moment he saw the property, he told me he had envisioned our future there. He dreamed of getting that calf nursery started some day and owning his own business. So I supported him. Even though I couldn't see it for myself.

After the wedding, Skyler and I moved in with the boys. It had taken a lot of work, but we were growing to love our little home. Tim had redone a lot of the inside. He ripped up carpet and sanded and stained the hardwood floors. He also took a window out of the bathroom that looked down on the stairs that led to our basement. He was able to make a wall there so that we could hang up a medicine cabinet, as the bathroom was extremely small and needed the space to be efficiently utilized. He did a lot of little things here and there with the plumbing, and his mom had done an awesome job of repainting every room in the house. Of course, there was also some serious cleaning involved. It is amazing what a fresh coat of paint can do for a home.

By the time everything was said and done, the kids absolutely loved their rooms.

There were still issues with insulation, and boy, I really hated windy days. We would try to keep the house warm by hanging up blankets and even went as far as to put an old mattress in front of the west side door. Yet we could always see the blankets swaying from the wind that was sneaking in. More than once, Tim and I would lie in bed arguing about who was going to jump out from beneath the warm comforter to turn off the lights, because the floor was not carpeted and would sting our toes to the touch from the cold. Looking back, I wonder why the last person in the room didn't just turn off the lights before crawling into bed.

The kids had the space heaters that Tim's parents had gotten us for Christmas, so they always had nice, toasty rooms upstairs. In the winter, we had a little snow pile in the corner on the inside of our entryway, and during the spring when it was raining, water leaking from the window slowly accumulated in a little puddle in our living room. But these were temporary problems, and we always found a way to handle them. Tim was good at fixing things, and if he couldn't quite figure one out, friends or family would stop by and offer suggestions.

We loved our home. Maybe mostly because it was ours.

Tim was still working with hogs and I was still working for the county, but I had a new position as a social worker. I also did transcription, granting me the ability to start working from home a couple days a week. The hard part was that Skyler and Nathan went to different schools, but we made it work.

In Tim's free time, he continued to work on getting the calf nursery up and running. Until finally, one day, it was ready for business. The only holdup now was that Tim was struggling with finding someone to do business with.

I was still feeling great, experiencing no symptoms from FM since I had gotten my stents. I was just doing yearly checkups to make sure all was well and that my stents were staying open. At my visit in 2009, I asked Dr. Youness if I could have more children. He told me, "Why not? Go live your life." He again reaffirmed what he had told me back in 2007, that I was going to be around for a long time. Then he joked, "At least FM won't be what kills you anytime soon."

Due to Tim's surgery and all of my crazy health issues, there was a significant chance that we would struggle to have more children anyway. Right before we were married, I had been in to see my gynecologist for some heavy periods and lower abdominal pain. He had informed me that due to some unexplained damage to my fallopian tubes (which were essentially shriveled up, so to speak), there was a good chance I would have a hard time getting pregnant. My heart had ached at that news, because I loved Tim and wanted to be able to build upon our family with him. I knew God had brought us together for a reason, but it pained me to think I might be the reason he couldn't have any more kids. He was such an amazing father; I didn't want to be the one denying him more.

I had given Tim a chance to back out of the wedding, but he didn't take it. He explained that as much as he wanted to have more children, he loved me far more than the idea of more kids, and he was willing to risk never having any more at all, so long as he could still have me. Skyler and Nathan would be enough for us, if that was God's plan.

After I had the all clear from the doctor, we tried for several months to get pregnant. Every month I went through as many as six to ten pregnancy tests, the suspense driving me to madness. I wanted a baby more than anything and was heartbroken every time the tests came back negative. I started to wonder if maybe God didn't have any plans for more children in our lives. Perhaps our little family of four just wasn't meant to expand. I tried to remember what we had decided, that Skyler and Nathan could be enough. And they were; we each loved both children with full and open hearts. They were ours, together.

Still, my heart ached to have just one more with this man I loved.

We decided to go camping in Yellowstone for our family vacation that year, as we had done so much camping from the time Tim and I met. The kids were both ecstatic!

Each of the grandmas set the kids up with fun goodies for the car, and we drove seventeen hours straight through the night. From the minute we entered the gate to Yellowstone, our vacation was full of excitement. We were fortunate enough to see grizzly bears prowling in the grass and crossing the road. Moose and elk made appearances. And we got surrounded by buffalo while sitting in the truck.

Through binoculars, we were also able to see wolves playing with each other and rolling around in the brush. And as we were driving through the park one night, we spotted a coyote that prompted us to pull over to the side of the road. We rolled down our windows and heard coyotes yipping back and forth to each other. It was a very cool experience for all of us.

We also hiked some of the trails and saw geysers and Old Faithful. The weather was beautiful, and at night, deer would brush up against our tents. Time went by fast, and we didn't ever want to leave.

On our drive home, we stopped at Mount Rushmore around 9:30 at night. Surprisingly, this seemed to be one of the highlights for the kids as we went up in the middle of a thunderstorm and the power had gone out. The lightning brightened the sky, and we were able to see all four presidents through the streaks and flashes from above. It was one of those vacations we will each always remember.

After returning home and getting back into the routine of things, I took yet another pregnancy test. It was more out of habit than anything. I had truly started to convince myself this would never happen. But finally, I had a positive result show up! I was so excited that I couldn't wait to tell Tim.

I went outside and started walking toward him, carrying the pregnancy test behind my back. I was trying to contain my excitement as I approached him and said, "Looks like you're going to be a daddy." I took the test from behind my back and showed it to him. I will never forget the smile and look in his eyes when he heard the news. His eyes were actually sparkling, and his smile melted me. From that reaction, I knew yet again that he would be a wonderful father.

On May 7, 2010, God blessed us with Leah Lavonne Lalk. I was convinced that she was going to be a boy, as the pregnancy was pretty hard on me and I was always sick—very different from my pregnancy with Skyler. Certain smells made it worse, and Tim was a smoker, which was one of my triggers. He did a great job of not smoking in the house or in the vehicles, and he even avoided smoking around the kids and me at all costs. But I could still smell it. So on February 14, 2010, he quit in the hopes that I would not get as sick anymore. That was the best thing he did for our family and for his own health. It also proved to me, yet again, how committed he was to being the man I needed him to be.

Leah was absolutely gorgeous. She had so much hair that she could have had pigtails coming home straight from the hospital. She was Daddy's little princess from the day he laid eyes upon her. Tim and I thanked God every day for blessing us with this little miracle.

Shortly after Leah was born, Tim finally got his business started custom-raising calves. I was so happy for him, as this was what we had been praying for and what he had worked extremely hard for. But we found out very fast how much work it really was, and he became instantly busy. Thankfully, we had great family support and Tim's dad played a huge part in getting the business started. He was always letting Tim borrow the tools or equipment that he needed. He also did all of the physical work alongside Tim and showed Tim how to do things whenever he had questions or needed advice.

My dad even came and helped Tim with the chores, taking on whatever tasks he needed help with. I was still working full-time and caring for a newborn, but I helped where I could as well.

Things were really moving fast, and I think we both began to feel overwhelmed. I had grown up in a household where

I was used to my parents being home by 4:30 p.m., having supper, then watching the news and just enjoying each other's company the rest of the evening. I had also grown up where weekends were a time to relax and be with the family. Tim was working seven days a week and seemed to be working all day long. He wasn't getting in from his job until after 8:00 most nights, so it was up to me to get the kids fed, bathed, finished with their homework, and off to bed. This was on top of trying to do my job at home and keeping up with the housework. When Tim came in, I would heat him up dinner as well and maybe start some laundry. If we were lucky, we were in bed by midnight most nights, only to get back up by 6:00 the next morning to do it all over again. I was nowhere used to these long days.

Everything about this work was hard and beautiful and exciting and scary. Tim had introduced me to a whole new lifestyle, and I loved him for that. But while I was extremely grateful for how far God had brought us, it was also getting harder to handle everything.

I wasn't sure how much longer we could both continue juggling everything up in the air.

I had not been to Dr. Youness for my regular follow-ups during my pregnancy due to the dye and medications needed for the procedure. I held off until Leah was about six months old, as the medications would have also interrupted breastfeeding. I knew that if they did have to open my stents, I would need to take it easy and not be able to lift her for a couple of days. So I waited until she was a little older, despite the fact that I was starting to experience some symptoms again. I had been very tired and was getting headaches, but I kept excusing that as being part of having a baby and just being tired and worn out from the long days and nights. It was easy to ignore my body when we had so much else going on.

In December 2010, when I called to schedule my follow-up, I learned that Dr. Youness had left the hospital and was no longer there. This was disappointing, particularly when it turned out my stents did need to be opened after all. This was the first time I had to have angioplasty with ballooning since I had gotten the stents back in 2007.

Another doctor did the procedure, which was very similar to when I had gotten the stents in. The nurses put a PICC line in each of my arms and this time one PICC line in one hand, and then I was rolled to the operating room where I was switched over to another long, thin table with my arms out. I was offered a warm blanket, which I graciously accepted because the room was freezing. And then they began wiping the cold dye on my arms from shoulder to elbow, creating something like a tent over my head with a blue tarp. I was once again given medications to help me relax but not put me completely to sleep.

Just like during the first surgery, small incisions were made in both of my upper arms and I could feel something going through my veins, as if there was a worm crawling around in there. I giggled as the catheter got to my underarms. It was a nervous giggle, as going through this procedure for the first time since I had gotten my stents three years before was a reminder that I still had FM. And while I had been living with very few symptoms the past few years, it was all sneaking back up on me. I didn't like needing to be here.

I felt the uncomfortable pressure in my chest and then I was done and told to follow up in six months. I had to wait an hour to make sure I didn't get sick and handled the sedation without issue, but then I was released. I wasn't feeling the best, and actually needed Tim to pull over on the drive so I could get sick on the side of the road. I figured that was all part of recovering. I had no idea this would soon become a regular routine.

Within a day or two after returning home, I was feeling lousy and getting the headaches and chest pressure again. Basically, I was experiencing the same symptoms I had been dealing with before the procedure—almost like it hadn't been done at all. I doubted myself, but after talking to Tim, I decided to call the doctor. I questioned whether it was possible that my stents could have closed so quickly. After all, he had just done the procedure. He said that no, I must have a cold or something else going on. And that was that.

After less than a month of battling the nasty symptoms and still feeling terrible, I knew something had to be wrong, so I called to make an appointment. To my surprise (and gratitude), Dr. Youness was back. I hadn't felt overly comfortable with the other doctor and was excited to see someone who knew my case.

I had been getting frequent headaches and chest pressure since my last procedure. I had also been sleeping on the couch, which tended to ease the pressure in my chest. During the days when I was home, I would wear the loosest-fitting shirt I could find. My chest was so full of pressure and pain that I always felt like my clothing was squeezing me, even though that wasn't the case. I went back and saw Dr. Youness, only to discover that my stents had indeed closed. So I was prepped for the procedure.

Everything went just as it had before and I was told to follow up in March to ensure that the stents stayed open this time. I was able to avoid getting sick at the hospital from the medication they used during the procedure, but once more I needed Tim to pull over on the drive home.

It was after this second procedure since Leah had been born that I asked Dr. Youness again if I could still have children. Despite everything going on, Tim and I still wanted to have another baby. But this time, Dr. Youness appeared more hesitant. He simply replied, "I can't tell you not to have children."

It was the one time I did not share with my parents all of the details from my visit.

After my checkup in July, my stents were still open, and this time, I had been feeling better for a few months. So Tim and I decided now was a good time as any to begin trying for another baby. And again, I was getting anxious waiting for it to happen. Until one morning, I got the very faint positive I had been waiting for. And I was so excited to tell him.

I put Leah, who was just over a year old now, into a T-shirt that said, "Big Sister," and had her go out to talk to Daddy. He was, of course, out in the calf nursery. His dad would often joke that Tim needed a cot out there for as much work as he was doing in that building.

We walked up and he started rambling on about the cows. Then he was talking to Leah but not really noticing what she was wearing. It took him a while, but he finally read her shirt and smiled. Then he kissed me on the cheek and joked that he'd better get back to working, with one more mouth to feed. We were happy. This was what we had been praying for.

Shortly after that, however, I began spotting and became concerned. I went to the doctor and my pregnancy hormone levels were very low. She reported that I was having a miscarriage. I crumbled into tears then and there. I was just not able to understand why God had to make everything so difficult for me. Why couldn't my life just be filled with things going the way they were supposed to go?

My plan as a child had been to choose a career that I loved, get married, have four children—all two years apart—and live in Hawaii while growing peanut-butter cups. Yes, really. I was going to grow peanut-butter cups.

I mean, had that been too much to ask? This was my life, my plan. I was even willing to give up on the peanut-butter cups, if only I could just have the rest.

In September 2011, we went camping on another family vacation, even as I was still spotting. This was our first family vacation with Leah and the first days off that Tim had taken from his business since he started it in 2010. We were so blessed and thankful that my dad and his dad were willing to do chores while we were gone, as we really needed this chance to get away and relax. Tim was such a hard worker, and I was starting to feel like all I was doing was causing more stress and expenses to him because of my medical issues. We needed this time as a family.

We went to Fenske Lake Cabins for a week, which was right by the Boundary Waters. We usually tented when we camped, but due to Leah still being so young, and not really knowing how she would do in a tent, we decided to try out a cabin. Despite the miscarriage, I did try to enjoy myself for Leah, Nathan, Skyler, and Tim. I felt awful with some cramping and would fight back tears as the thought that I was losing a baby constantly cluttered my mind. It didn't help that I was also feeling lousy again with the chest pressure and headaches. My heart was broken in a million pieces. But I was trying to hold it together.

Tim got up one morning before the kids to take the boat out and do some fishing, so I walked out to the dock with him. He loaded up his fishing gear, grabbed his coffee, gave me a kiss, and then he was off. I sat on the bench at the end of our dock and listened to the low rumble of his trolling motor off in the distance.

Looking around, I suddenly felt this overwhelming sense of calmness and peace. I was surrounded by green pine trees and a clear-blue lake, with the orange sunrise coming up and reflecting off the water. It left me breathless. The view was amazing and so crisp and clear. I saw how wonderful and big God was, and I was surrounded by His beauty. Seeing all that He had created made me wonder how I could have any doubt that He didn't know what He was doing with me. In that moment, I felt as though God had wrapped His arms around me to let me know He was with me and that everything was going to be okay.

I was finally accepting that I had lost the baby, but when we returned back home, I went in to have my levels checked again. This time, they had doubled, like they should have with a healthy pregnancy. My nurses were confused, and again my hopes were high as I shared the news with Tim. I went to the doctor, and before he could say anything, I responded full of excitement. But I also told him I was greatly concerned, as I had consumed four Diet Mountain Dews while on vacation—assuming I was no longer pregnant. I was afraid that all the caffeine might have hurt the baby. When I was pregnant with Leah and Skyler, the doctors had told me I should be a poster mom because I did everything by the book. I managed my blood sugars perfectly, took my vitamins, ate healthy, and never had caffeine or alcohol.

My doctor now had a shy, amused smile on his face as he took in my panic, but then his smile dropped. He explained that I had an ectopic pregnancy. He went on to say that although my numbers had gone up, they were nowhere near where they should have been. I joked, explaining that my body was beyond messed up, so it might be possible that I had a healthy pregnancy and my body was just messing up the numbers. That was how much hope I still had.

He paused, but then he explained that with the bleeding, he was certain this was an ectopic pregnancy. He told me that an ectopic pregnancy could not be viable and would need to be terminated, as it was a risk to my life to allow it to continue.

My heart again sank. Why would God allow me to get my hopes up? What kind of sick joke was this? And what lesson was I supposed to learn by having to terminate a pregnancy I so desperately wanted? The doctor explained that this was medically necessary and that there was no way the baby would survive. He told me that not terminating would inevitably mean losing my own life. This wasn't an abortion, because the pregnancy could not be viable in my tube, where it was currently implanted. But in my heart, it all just felt wrong.

My emotions were going up and down. I could not stop crying and thinking about the baby I was losing. Over the next month, every time I got in my car, the song *Blessings* came on. I knew that God was still with me and had a better plan, although I couldn't help but wish His plan didn't have to hurt so much.

Tim and I decided that maybe this wasn't the right time to be adding to our family. Plus we were still mourning the loss of our baby. We decided to stop trying.

Tim continued to stay extremely busy with his cattle business. I was still driving Skyler to school and working in Waverly, while Nathan was getting on the bus and going to his elementary school every day in Sumner. There was beginning to be a lot of strain on us as a family, because it felt like we were still two separate families. Our routines had us moving in opposite directions. And I wasn't totally sure how to bring us all back together again.

I started to work more at home, as I was still doing part-time social work and part-time transcribing. I was going into the office three days a week, and the drive was still long on those few days, especially in the winter months.

The house was also getting too small for the five of us, but it was so convenient because we were close to Tim's family and his work. His mom and sister Brenda were awesome at helping out with the kids whenever we needed it, and it was wonderful having them just minutes away. Plus the kids loved playing with their "crazy cousins," who were always stopping over to give Skye and Nathan a hard time about something.

We had been throwing around the idea of moving for a while though and had actually seen an acreage for sale right outside Waverly. We toured it a couple of times and had fallen in love with it. While Tim was reminding me that the house we had seen was his dream home, it felt like a huge decision, as moving would have involved Nathan to change schools. We agreed to pray about it, wanting to do what was best for our family and not rush the decision.

Then just like that, God blessed us with another positive pregnancy test. I was nervous from the loss but hopeful and unable to contain my excitement as soon as we learned that everything looked good.

On the day that we were going to tell Tim's family, his brother and his wife beat us to the punch. They had two children already and were pregnant again. I looked at Tim, making sure he knew to keep his mouth shut. We were not going to steal their thunder and announce anything on their special day.

I was so excited for them but also for myself; it would be so much fun to be pregnant at the same time as my sister-in-law. Meanwhile, Tim's other sister (who lived out of state) was also pregnant. There were going to be a lot of additions to the family!

We waited another week before we finally told his family. In the meantime, I was also talking to my closest friend and coworker, Dusty, who told me she was pregnant the same day I found out I was. We were so excited, having been friends for nearly a decade. Being pregnant at the same time as so many of the women I already loved and cared for was a blessing I hadn't even thought to hope for.

Tim was pushing away at his job, working long days, and it felt like we barely saw him. We decided to do another family vacation before the baby came. This time, we opted to go back to Minnesota.

I was about seven months' pregnant, and nobody could believe I was going to camp in a tent of my own free will. But minus Tim having to blow up the air mattress every night and me barely being able to get off the stupid thing in the mornings, everything went great.

We found a place right on Moose Lake off the Boundary Waters, and again the beauty was just breathtaking. The kids had so much fun jumping out of the boat, fishing, and swimming. At night, they were bouncing with excitement, yet we could sense a bit of fear from them as well. They would move closer to sit by us when we heard the wolves howling in the distance.

The best part of that trip was how Tim was able to relax and enjoy himself away from the business. It felt so nice to have us all focused completely on our little family.

On our last night, there was a chance of storms so we decided to pack up and go into town, not wanting to repeat the storm experience from one of our first camping trips together. We stayed at a little lodge, and the kids quickly decided they preferred that style of camping to tents. They loved the food at the restaurant and the huge game room where they could play anything they wanted. Not to mention the big swimming pool we had all to ourselves. It was such a nice vacation that we agreed we would take trips like this at least once a year. We had no idea then that it would be several years before we got to vacation again.

Asher Timothy Lalk was born on October 10, 2012, and wow did he have just as much hair as Leah. I was dilated by the time I got to the hospital, and after my water was broken, the doctor announced that I would go fast. I was not happy when the anesthesiologist got there too late for the epidural to kick in. Asher was born with me feeling everything.

All of that pain disappeared once we heard the cry of our newborn son. He was so adorable and was Mommy's boy from the minute I held him in my arms. His name, handpicked from the Bible, meant "blessing." And after everything the previous year had brought, he truly was a blessing. God had shown yet again how amazing and loving He was.

Asher's bilirubin levels were high shortly after he was born, so he was closely monitored. We were able to take him home with a heat blanket, but when that didn't work, he was readmitted to the hospital. There my little baby lay in an incubator with his little sunglasses, for days. I wasn't able to hold him, and I desperately yearned to. I cried so much for him, wondering how parents handled having a child with severe illnesses. This was just jaundice, and my heart ached watching him go through it. He was poked and picked on by nurses who sometimes were not compassionate at all. Both Tim and I asked them on several occasions to be gentler.

One horrible experience involved an extremely rude and heartless nurse who tried to draw blood. I was sitting out in the waiting room while Tim took Asher in, because I just couldn't stand to hold him down and hear him cry while they poked and squeezed his little foot. While sitting there, I heard my baby start screaming. He wasn't stopping. My heart was frantic and I was trying everything in my power to stay in my seat.

Finally, enough was enough. I stood up and charged back toward the lab, only to see Tim exiting, his face red with anger. He was carrying Asher in his arms with the white bandage dangling from our baby's foot. Tim said that the nurse was rude and impatient and, instead of taking her time to pump the blood from Asher's foot, had poked him three times in different places. She was actually going to poke him again when Tim stopped her. She had not used anything to warm his foot to allow the blood to flow better, even though that was what all the other nurses did. She had even attempted to put a needle in Asher's arm to get the blood.

Tim looked at me and said, with his voice cracking, "He's so little. I have to stand up for him, because he can't."

We went up to pediatrics where he had been delivered, and the nurses were able to help us by only poking Asher once, getting more than enough blood for what they needed. Our heart broke for our little boy, but I admired Tim and was so proud of him for standing up for Asher.

After more praying, Tim and I made a decision to switch churches. A new pastor had taken over. He was great, but we just didn't feel the connection with the church that we once attended. One Sunday, we decided to attend a church a few towns over. Hearing the first sermon from Pastor John, we knew this was where God wanted us to be. This would be our new church home. The drive was longer from our house, about forty-five minutes both ways, but we really felt a connection and decided to start attending.

Tim and I also continued to pray and discussed buying the house we had looked at before. There were now six of us in our very tiny, three-bedroom farmhouse. While we had tried fixing up part of the basement for Skyler to sleep in, she seemed nervous there. At this point, she was basically sharing Leah's room upstairs. Asher was sleeping in his Pack 'n Play in the living room, and sometimes in our bedroom, depending on the night, because colic had set in shortly after we brought him home. That did not help with anything.

Nathan actually seemed excited about switching schools, which was something we had struggled with. Tim seemed ready to live somewhere other than where he worked. I reminded him of how nice it was to be able to look out the window to see that everything was okay with the building and the cows, but he explained that was sometimes the worst thing. He told me he was at his job twelve hours a day, and sometimes more. When he came home, that was already all he could think about. It was that much worse when he could see the cows right out the window. He felt like he never got away from work.

Amid all our praying, we looked around at church one Sunday and saw the Realtor who had shown us the house sitting a row over. We called her the next day. Although Tim had become instantly successful with his job and we had a good income rolling in, we still threw out some low numbers, knowing we could not afford the asking price. We figured as much as Tim loved the house, it was worth a shot to offer what we were comfortable with and see what happened.

It turned out we were meant to have that home.

In February 2013, we moved into our new home, and the kids were finally all in one school system. We prayed a lot for everyone to adjust well to the move, and our prayers seemed to be answered. I had to drive much less between home and work now. Skyler was able to have friends from school over more often. Nathan was doing great in his new school, made friends right away, and was happy for the change. It all seemed to work out perfectly.

Everything was exactly as it should be, except for my health. I continued to feel okay, but I knew my body well and knew I would need to have the angioplasty again to open my stents soon. We were still too busy for me to be down a day or two to recover, so I continued putting it off as long as I could.

I finally went back in for my first checkup after Asher was around four months old, and my suspicions were confirmed. I had to get my stents opened.

I was overwhelmed with keeping up with work, the house, the laundry, the cooking, and the kids. I didn't feel like I had time to keep going in for doctors' appointments. I was starting to lose focus on God and was getting wrapped up in the busy everyday schedule of life.

And that was when my health began to drastically deteriorate.

In July 2013, I went in for my regular angioplasty. I knew, yet again, from the headaches and chest pressure I was having that he would have to open my stents again. And I was right, making this my second procedure since Asher had been born the previous October. Dr. Youness did the procedure and then I was on my way.

The problem this time was I didn't wind up feeling any relief. I got through the weekend but still felt horrible. My chest hurt to the point of not being able to wear a bra. My shirts again felt like they were squeezing me, restricting my air, and my head would not stop pounding.

I was miserable, and I was getting that cough I hadn't had in a long time. Just as I was fighting that off, I noticed a bunch of little veins all over my neck and chest that could probably have glowed in the dark. I showed Tim, and his reaction immediately proved to me that this was something to be concerned about.

I called Dr. Youness and he asked me to come in. I was expecting to just do the regular angioplasty and balloon, but when they went in to balloon me, they discovered that I had a blood clot in my upper right chest. I was immediately admitted to the hospital.

That really caught me off guard, and it's possible I didn't react as well as I should have. I was on medication to dissolve the clot and was to be on complete bed rest. I was mostly fine with that, until I realized it meant I had to lie flat on my back. I wasn't even allowed to get up to use the bathroom.

I was in my thirties and told the nurse I was not going to use a bedpan, so she tried to compromise by offering me a commode right by my bed. I was feeling stubborn and frustrated. I said if I couldn't use an actual bathroom, I would just hold it for as long as I could. I know the nursing staff was exasperated with me, but what they didn't understand was how protective I was feeling of my independence. I had two babies at home. I was used to changing diapers. And I was not about to let someone else do the same level of dirty work for me. Plus I wasn't feeling dizzy and was sure I could walk ten feet to the bathroom. I just hated being told I couldn't do something that seemed so simple to me.

Eventually, it was my regular nurse, the one I had been seeing for years, who took up my cause. She got Dr. Youness to agree to bed rest with "bathroom privileges." She whispered that I must be special, because he never let anyone out of bed on the medications I was on. Then she explained the importance of not falling or bumping any part of my body that might cause internal bruising and bleeding. I was extremely grateful, but my mom was baffled, unable to understand how, with everything else going on, this was the battle I had decided to fight.

What she was missing was how much I needed even the small victories.

After that first night on bed rest, I was again wheeled into the operating room. The cold dye was applied, and the small incisions in my arms were made, only to find that the blood clot was not gone. I was sent back to my hospital room to wait until the afternoon. That was when I went back a second time to do the whole procedure all over again. The clot was still not completely dissolved, so I had to stay another night.

I was able to keep the tears from flowing until I got back to my room. My arms were sore and stung, as if someone had been pinching me with the tip of their fingers and not letting up. On top of that, I hated to be spending another night away from my family. Although it was a lot of driving back and forth for Tim, I was so thankful that he had at least come back to stay with me in between chores. I told him not to worry about staying overnight though, because we were in a room that was shared with another woman and all that separated us was a curtain. There was no privacy and really no place for him to sleep. Still, I could see on Tim's face that he did not want to leave, but I insisted.

When he finally did leave, my heart sank. While I had told him to go, I just desperately wanted to be leaving with him. This was not where I wanted to be. The first night had been hard, as I lay in my bed wondering what was happening to me. But the second night was almost unbearable.

I had been through three procedures in two days, with yet another one still on the books for the following day. I had a catheter going through my arm into my chest, so I was supposed to keep it as straight as possible. I would get scolded by one of the nurses if I bent it ever so slightly to help sit myself up in bed, which was also a no-no. There were so many tubes and wires, and the lady I was sharing the room with kept trying to have the most bizarre conversations with me. She was obviously on good pain medications.

Lying in bed all night by myself, with nurses coming in and out every hour to check my vitals, made sleep impossible. None of this was helped by the yelling and screaming from other patients down or across the hall or the bad thoughts creeping in my head from my original diagnosis. I kept going back to 2002, when I had been given ten years to live. FM was starting to affect my life on a more frequent basis now, and I couldn't help but think maybe the doctors had been right. It had been eleven years since I'd been diagnosed, and I was feeling awful every day now. Maybe my time really was about to end.

I cried a lot and was so thankful to see Tim in the morning. I had been independent for so long, but now that I had Tim in my life, I really was relying on him. Cliché or not, he was my rock, my shoulder to cry on. And through it all, he still found ways to make me laugh.

Finally, on my third day in the hospital, I went back to the operating room. My arms were prepped, and thankfully, the blood clot was gone. Dr. Youness put two more stents in my SVC to help keep it open, meaning I now had six stents in total. I was put on a blood thinner, along with baby aspirin, and told to come back in three months.

The headaches and chest pressure were a lot better, but I began to get short of breath and feel extremely tired. I questioned myself, wondering if the stents were closed again. But these were not my usual symptoms, so I wasn't entirely sure what to think.

I was getting so tired throughout the day, and was becoming so short of breath going up and down the stairs, that I would have to sit and take a break halfway up them. I was also getting so tired at work that I needed to come home and actually lie down. I had never taken naps before and had always been able to function on less than six hours of sleep, so this new shift was difficult to understand.

I was also getting a lot of heartburn, which I had never struggled with before, except for during my pregnancy with Asher. Now, it was so severe that I was actually throwing up most nights.

I still didn't want to acknowledge that something truly scary could be going on. So I put it all off as just getting older, possibly not being able to eat certain foods. But no matter what I ate, the heartburn was there. So then I tried to convince myself that maybe I just couldn't eat as late as I had been. But eating earlier made no difference.

Then I started getting heart palpitations. And still, I ignored.

As if these new symptoms weren't enough, I also began getting extremely dry hands and my fingernails were beginning to dent and look deformed. My hands were at the point where they were bleeding all of the time from the deep cracks and cuts, which would just pulsate from pain if I accidentally hit or jammed them on something. Typing for my job only aggravated them more. My hands were so deformed and sore that I could barely function using them. As painful as it was, this was at least something I felt like I could deal with. So back to my family doctor I went, only to be referred to a dermatologist.

The dermatologist quickly explained that this flare-up could easily have come from the stents, as those were foreign objects. People's bodies have a way of reacting oddly to things like that. My FM doctors didn't agree, but it didn't really matter what the reason was. I just wanted it fixed.

I was diagnosed with severe eczema and ordered to begin light therapy three times a week. I had to drive to Cedar Falls for the sessions, where I put on the same dark sunglasses you get after an eye exam. And then I would put my hands into this little machine for maybe forty or fifty seconds. I was driving forty-five minutes, three days a week, for fifty seconds of treatment. Which would have been fine if it worked, but it didn't. I felt like I was falling apart. I just wanted to go to one appointment that was considered a routine checkup without having to be referred to a specialist.

On top of my health concerns, Leah and Asher were ending up at the doctor almost weekly it seemed. Leah was getting routinely sick and spiking high fevers and Asher was getting constant ear infections. If I was not at home due to my health, I was at home because of sick kids. Thankfully, my boss was extremely accommodating, allowing me to work from home as much as I needed. But it was still hard to be dealing with so much sickness. This may have been the norm for the toddler years, but adding my ailments on top of it just made things more difficult.

For some reason, I also started thinking about my initial FM diagnosis. I had been told back then that my lung was only functioning at 25 percent. Talking to Tim one night, I wondered aloud if Dr. Youness had checked that when he was working on my SVC.

It was during that conversation that I first saw the strain all of our health concerns were putting on Tim. He tried to be at the appointments for the kids, but it was becoming so common that there was no way he could continue to be at every one. He was weighed down with worry for me, as he watched me struggling physically and emotionally, trying hard to handle everyday activities and duties. I would take breaks after carrying a basket of laundry upstairs or have to sit after carrying Asher across the room, and fear would cross his face. I was getting worse and I hated that I was feeling this way, but I hated even more that it was affecting him. I wanted so much to be strong, but instead I just broke down crying. It was all starting to be too much.

And then one night, Tim had a breakdown of his own. He said there was no way he could do this without me, crying that the kids needed me. That they all needed me, so nothing could happen to take me away.

We were both feeling so helpless.

For whatever reason though, after finally letting all that out, Tim really began to step up. He had always been my rock, but now he was determined to keep us all afloat. I was becoming the weak one, and he was the one standing up for me when I couldn't.

I was sick of being sick and starting to get bitter and grumpy. Tim could see me giving up my fight and worked to lead me through yet another dark time in my life. Except this time, I was not alone. He was with me.

Even when we were all knocked down once more.

Tim's brother Aaron was diagnosed with leukemia on September 24, 2013. I cried a lot with my husband, as we could not begin to imagine what Aaron and his family were going through.

They had three children. Haley was six, Jace was four, and Garret would be celebrating his first birthday on September 28. Our hearts broke for them. Tim, especially, was struggling with what this all meant. He had been so busy at work, and my medical expenses were piling up. Between that and the normal concerns that come with raising four kids, we both were sad, stressed, and overwhelmed, which translated into us taking some of that out on each other.

We had been arguing over things that didn't really matter in the long run. Then Aaron was diagnosed with cancer, and the outcome did not look good. It all just felt so ... hard. So much harder than it should be.

One night, Tim sat with me on the couch and held my hand while crying and asking why he was busting his butt so hard with work if life could just change in the blink of an eye. He asked why we should stress over things that really didn't matter in the end. We needed to be enjoying each other, enjoying life, to appreciate and be thankful for all that we had, because everything could be taken away in the blink of an eye.

Aaron continued to be in the hospital week after week, going through rounds of chemo. All of the siblings had tested to see if they were a match for Aaron, in the hopes that he might be eligible for a bone-marrow transplant. One of his sisters was an exact match, and while we were all so grateful for this, I could tell Tim was disappointed he wasn't a match. He really wanted to be there for Aaron and felt like he had let him down again.

In the meantime, my symptoms continued to worsen. I knew by this point that it wasn't a result of my SVC, but I didn't like thinking about what else could be wrong. So I continued to wait until my routine appointment rolled around. I would snap at Tim when he asked how I was feeling, sharply replying with, "I'm fine." Which wasn't fair, but I also didn't see the point in repeatedly telling him or my mom or friends about how crappy I really was feeling. They couldn't do anything about it, so what was the point?

Part of my being so guarded was also the result of knowing that some of my family and friends still didn't seem to fully understand the severity of my disease. I felt like I was dying and was starting to realize that the doctors were right: this disease would eventually kill me. These stupid stents were just making me feel better temporarily, but the outcome would not be any different. I was just being made to feel comfortable until I died, and frankly, there was nothing comfortable about this disease. But explaining that to people, trying to make them understand when I otherwise looked fine, was tiring. It just made more sense to not talk about it at all, even with the people who did understand and care.

I went to see Dr. Youness in October. My SVC stents were not closed, but I finally admitted to him that something else was wrong. I told him about my symptoms and he agreed that by this point I knew my body well enough to understand when something wasn't right. I asked if he could tell if my lung had experienced any more damage. He suggested I see my pulmonologist, explaining that he or she would be able to look into that further.

The look on both my and Tim's faces must have said it all. It was then that Dr. Youness realized I wasn't seeing any other doctor. He was it.

He immediately said that with my history of FM, and the issues with breathing, I needed to see a pulmonologist right away. He started pulling up referrals as we sat there, waiting, trying not to be scared.

I found my FM support group yet again on Facebook. Even after so many years away, I still recognized some of the same old names. There were a lot of new names as well. Three of the individuals I had previously known in the group had died since I last checked in. There were also several other original members who had been doing mostly okay back then but were really struggling now.

I began to share my story, feeling for perhaps the first time like I really did have a lot in common with these people. More than I wished to, as wonderful as they were. Who would want to be a part of this club after all?

I began turning to the group for advice, support, and to just vent my frustrations with FM. It was amazing how much we were alike in terms of what we were dealing with, even as our lives were all so different. I had been able to get stents to help my symptoms, but many of them had never been given the same option. Some of them were also having surgeries or some form of antifungal treatment that my doctors had said was not an option for me.

But one thing seemed to have remained the same, even after all these years. There was still very little in the way of information or treatment options for this disease that would inevitably kill us all.

Dr. Youness offered to make a referral to a pulmonologist; however, I decided I would try to find a local doctor first in order to reduce driving. I was sent back to my regular family doctor, who knew of my disease and was always very apologetic that I had FM. The hope was that he might be able to make the best referral for a local pulmonologist. The first time he met with me as a patient, after the kids had been born, he stated that from looking at me all this time, he had no idea that I had such a horrible disease. He said I looked great.

I remember kind of laughing to myself, thinking that was the problem. I didn't look sick, so nobody ever believed how miserable I really was feeling.

My doctor ordered some tests and then made the referral back to Iowa City, as he did not feel any local pulmonologists would be able to provide what I truly needed. I did a CT scan and an echocardiogram and then took the results to my referral.

This doctor reviewed my tests and confirmed that there were some abnormalities in my heart as well as that my right lung function was not good. It was so nice to talk with a doctor who knew what FM was and who believed me when I tried to explain how awful I was feeling. He stated that with this disease, there was no cure and they basically had to treat my symptoms as they came up, while doing the least amount of harm to my body as possible.

He reported that most likely I would need to stent my pulmonary artery, prompting a referral to a cardiologist who specialized in just such a surgery. I left the hospital crying, because again everyone was thinking this was great news—that I could just get a stent and feel better. Tim even said he liked that theory of treating my symptoms as they arose, with the goal being to produce the least amount of damage.

What they didn't seem to understand was that none of this would cure me. I was still dying. This disease would still eventually take my life. So it felt like I was just waiting around until I started having more problems. How was that good news? I was getting so frustrated and not caring anymore; part of me just wanted to give up. Looking back, that was so selfish of me. I had a family who needed me to fight. I was not trusting that God would take care of me. But I was just ... so ... tired.

Back to Iowa City the next day for my apartment with the cardiologist. I cried the entire way. I hated the anticipation of these appointments even more than the painful and uncomfortable procedures that I would most likely have to endure. It was just a constant reminder that I did have a life-threatening disease, but now with so many more problems. The "deadline" I had been given from the Mayo Clinic back in the beginning was just becoming more and more real, as all the doctors in Iowa City agreed that I was dying. It was always in the back of my head. I couldn't shove those negative thoughts out.

The cardiologist I was seeing also knew a lot about FM, as he had treated other patients with the same condition. Actually, two people from my FM group were seeing him as well.

I had been under the impression that we were talking to him about setting up the procedure to get a new stent, but he wasn't in a rush to get there. He wanted to make sure he knew exactly what he was dealing with, so once again my appointment in Iowa City turned into a long day of test after test. From doing a physical exam, he appeared very intrigued by the fact that the second beat of my heart was louder than the first. Apparently this was very uncommon, so he had two more med students listen to my heart as well.

I had learned very early on with this disease that special and unique were never good things.

Once all the testing was done, the doctor confirmed that my FM was progressing. I blinked my eyes, shaking my head a little in disbelief, and then I started crying from the word "progressing."

In 2007, a doctor had told me the disease looked to have been "dying out." He told me that most of the damage had already occurred and now it was just about treating the symptoms. I had believed that. I had lived my life sure that the worst was over. And now, it was back.

I sat there as the cardiologist explained that this disease had a mind of its own. It could start fast then slow down. It could start slow and then progress fast. There was just no way to determine how it was going to affect each individual person.

He also confirmed that my right lung had gotten worse and was basically useless. So he was worried that my heart and left lung were under too much strain due to working overtime.

The tests did show that I now had minor pulmonary arterial hypertension, yet another rare disease caused by my FM. The cardiologist confirmed that he would put a stent in my right pulmonary artery, hoping to open it up and relieve some of the pressure and strain that was being put on my left lung and the left side of my heart.

He told me that my lung had been "significantly bad back then" and questioned why I hadn't been seeing a pulmonologist all along. I reminded him that I had seen tons of doctors and that most of those doctors had told me I was dying and had no good news for me at all. I also pointed out that the doctors who didn't say I was dying simply had no clue about FM. So of course they didn't suggest that I come back to see them for any type of follow-ups. They didn't understand this disease in the first place. Plus once I got my SVC stents, a lot of my symptoms subsided for years. During those years, it was easy to pretend that everything was fine. That I was "cured."

As we walked out of the doctor's office, my emotions ran wild. I was so tired of the tests and the doctors and the stents. No matter what, something else was always showing up on the tests. It seemed like whenever one problem was taken care of, another would arise just in time to start the whole process all over again.

I was trying to stay positive, but I was being swallowed by emotions of fear, anger, and defeat. I knew each of the "fixes" was only temporary and that this would be something I dealt with for the rest of my life—however long that might be. It stung to know I would never feel as good as I once had and that I would always have to live with these physical limitations. I began crying uncontrollably, again, feeling so helpless and defeated. I was starting to wonder if it was really worth all of the medical bills, the discomfort, and the inconvenience of constant appointments. What was I going to leave my family with? A pile of debt and memories of a sick mom.

This had been going on for so long that I was even more anxious about how those outside our family must view me. Did they think I was some drama queen, the kind of person who always had to have something bad going on? Did they think I was making it all up or exaggerating the details? Being looked at like a hypochondriac made me cringe. I even tried to hide my symptoms and emotions, because it just wasn't worth the uncomfortable silence and looks that I got after describing my disease.

I was shocked and heartbroken that the FM was progressing. Obviously, this wasn't what I wanted. I wanted to be around to raise my kids. I wanted to be able to run after them. I wanted to live out my days with my husband. I wasn't one of those people who loved the drama. I hated all of this. I hated being sick, I hated feeling awful, and I hated that nothing seemed capable of helping me.

Yes, I knew there were people out there with plenty of harder struggles than what I was dealing with. And I knew I needed to try to be grateful. But I could also admit to feeling selfish. I wanted my life back. I didn't want to be going to the doctor all the time, having procedure after procedure done. I hated this disease, I hated everything about it, and I hated that I had to live with it.

I prayed one night, *Please, God, either kill me now or let me enjoy the years that I have left without these ridiculous procedures and wasted days at the hospital.*

I felt like a terrible mother, unable to play with my kids, forever restricted to bed with a throbbing headache or sharp, stabbing pains. So often too physically exhausted to do anything other than listen to them downstairs laughing and playing with their dad. I should have been down there with them.

What kind of wife was I that there were days I could barely have the house clean or dinner on the table? Tim was busting his butt at work, and I couldn't even handle preparing him dinner. My body wouldn't even allow me to do that most days.

All of these thoughts just flooded my mind. I couldn't help but feel horrible about myself. I was starting to hate myself, and I hated that FM was taking over my body.

Enough is enough. Don't drag it out anymore.

We got into the car to head home, knowing I was going to be getting new stents soon, and the song "This Is Where the Healing Begins" came on. God was definitely using music to talk to me throughout this whole horrific journey. But at the time, I really didn't care. All I could do was cry the whole way home, thinking that everyone I loved would be better off without me.

My surgery was set up for December. In the meantime, I did a lot of crying. I was scared because this procedure would be more involved than any of my previous ones had been. They would be going through the groin, and that sounded a lot worse than going through my arms, which had always been painful enough.

I felt hopeless. Tim continued to struggle as well, seeing his brother fight for his life against leukemia, while I was crying every night, wanting to give up my own fight. He continued to encourage me and tried to stay positive. He would say we needed to not be working as much and that it was time to start doing things as a family, enjoying our time together. But we both felt the stress and pressure of needing to keep everything afloat.

He was swamped at work from the brutal cold winter and missing days when he should have been there, because he was at every appointment with me. I was trying to hold onto my job, knowing we needed my income and not wanting to be responsible for any more debt as a result of this disease.

I also thought about his brother a lot. So many times throughout the years, when I had felt really bad and there seemed to be no help for me, I would think maybe I would have been better off having cancer instead of this horrible, incurable disease. Some cancers at least had treatments and cures, while FM had nothing to offer but measures to make me comfortable. But then, cancer hit too close to home. It was sickening and heartbreaking to watch Aaron and his family deal with this, and again I hated myself for thinking cancer would have been a better alternative to what I was dealing with.

Aaron has always had a great sense of humor, ever since I met him, and seeing how he applied that to dealing with his own health battle really made me think about my situation a lot. I liked to put on a brave front and not accept any help from anyone. I was especially quick to blow off my situation as no big deal, even though the disease was slowly killing me inside. I lied to myself, and to others, a lot about the severity of what I was dealing with. *I am fine, and I don't need anybody to take care of my babies, because I am their mommy and I am supposed to be able to be there for them, no matter what.*

With Aaron, while I will never understand what he was going through, I could see a bit of myself in how he was acting. He was quick to joke about the cancer, just as I always had a smart remark about FM. Our coping mechanisms were very similar.

One Sunday, Aaron was roughhousing with the nephews at a family dinner. From the look on his wife's and dad's faces, I assumed this was not something he was supposed to be doing. I had been there though in that position with my health where I just did what I wanted to do and did not take the limitations that were requested by the doctors seriously.

As a parent, all you want to do is pick up your kids and play with them. It was easy to discount the risks, because I just wanted to be a mom. I should have been able to play volleyball or basketball with Skye or Nathan without getting tremendous pressure in my chest. I should have been able to bend over and pick up toys from the floor without getting a head rush and passing out. I would skip appointments because I didn't want the reality that I really was sick to be thrust in my face. If I didn't go to the doctor, then as far as I was concerned, I was fine and just had to buck up and deal with the symptoms. I just needed to get in shape; it was that simple.

With Aaron, I finally got a different view of what Tim and my family must have felt when watching me push too hard. Tim and I wanted to do anything we could to help Aaron and his wife. We just wanted to be there for them if they needed us. But Aaron resisted the help.

While I could understand that he did not want to stop having fun and living his life, I could also see the dangers that could arise if he took the roughhousing too far or refused to wear his mask when he should have it on. We loved him and we just wanted him to be around for a long time. I guess I finally understood why Tim and my mom would get frustrated with me when I ignored my limitations as well. And while Tim and I were truly sincere and wanted to do whatever we could do to help Aaron and his family, I now too saw that our families were offering to help us for the same reasons.

I prayed a lot more for Aaron and his family than I did for myself. He was in the hospital for several months, not able to see his children or to be at home with his wife. His immune system was just too weakened to risk it. Then there were all of the physical and emotional strains he was going through, which nobody could ever begin to imagine. His cancer could have immediate consequences, whereas my disease was chronic and ongoing. But at least I had time.

I was suddenly grateful that while this disease was terrible to deal with, I was still able to be home with my family on the worst of my days. Aaron gave me perspective. I asked God so many times to forgive me for wishing my situation to be any different.

Tim and I continued to get our family to church just about every Sunday, even when I was struggling with my faith. Skyler and I had started to volunteer with the little ones at church, and that was something I always looked forward to. I was trying to reassure myself that God was still with me, although I often wondered if He was really with any of us.

My mom and dad had planned a trip to Florida, but they put it off until after my procedure. That really upset me. There had been so many other times in my life when they had been forced to do the same. Anytime they ever had to postpone anything, it was because of me. Trips that were canceled, plans that were postponed—I felt awful that they were always putting their lives on hold.

Still, when they met Tim and me in Iowa City on December 15, 2013, I was grateful to have them there. The doctors came in and introduced themselves, once more outlining the worst-case scenarios. The procedure was to take about two and a half hours. The plan was for them to open up my pulmonary artery. Once again, I was left saying my good-byes to my mom, my dad, and my husband. And once again, I couldn't help but fear this might be the last time I would see them.

The room was cold. The team of nurses and doctors were extremely nice, but they just weren't the same team I had always been used to with Dr. Youness. It was weird looking around and not seeing their familiar faces.

One of the nurses came over and asked me how I was. I told her I was fine. It was very apparent that I was not fine though, the stress likely written all over my face. So they started prepping me and told me they would give me some medications to help me relax.

I was so afraid of this procedure, knowing they would be dealing with my heart. It was very difficult to push back all of the what-ifs running through my brain. They continued to assure me that all of the worst-case scenarios we had reviewed were rare, but *I* was rare. *My case* was rare. I mean, hello! Fewer than six hundred people in the entire United States were diagnosed with fibrosing mediastinitis. So telling me the risks were rare didn't exactly make me feel better.

The nurse asked if I was feeling any of the sedation yet. Still trying to push my anxiety away, I told her no. That was the last thing I remember about being in the operating room.

I opened my eyes to find my mom staring down at me, a look of true appreciation and happiness on her face.

The surgery had ultimately taken five and a half hours to perform. I had gotten two stents in my pulmonary artery, allowing my right lung to go from functioning at less than 11 percent to 75 percent. The doctor explained how complicated my case was, but everyone was pleased with the results. I visited with Mom and Dad briefly, until they had to rush back to get our kids from day care. Tim kissed me on the forehead, and I went back to sleep.

The rest of the day was a blur. I was in and out of consciousness as various people came to visit. I vaguely remember the doctor coming in to talk to me, and Tim's mom, dad, and sister Cathy also stopped in to visit. I will tell you right now that narcotics and in-laws do not mix. I'm pretty sure I didn't shut up the entire time they were there, yet I still couldn't tell you what I talked to them about.

Cathy was in town to do the bone-marrow transplant, as she was an exact match for Aaron. That procedure would be happening within the next week. As much as I knew Tim had wanted the donor to be him, I was secretly grateful it hadn't been, if only because I knew I needed him now. We couldn't both be in recovery!

The next morning, I woke up to a slight pain in both sides of my groin. Tim explained they had needed to go in through both sides. After a light breakfast and reminders of all the silly things I had said and done while coming out of sedation, I was able to go home by noon. And as usual, we had to make a stop for me to get sick on the side of the road.

I was feeling good though. A little sore from the procedure, but definitely an improvement from before. I was even able to return to work about two weeks after my surgery. I wasn't getting short of breath going up and down the stairs anymore, and I wasn't having to take naps during the day. Even my heartburn was gone.

Thank You, God!

I still noticed a heart palpitation here and there, but nothing like I had experienced before my stents. And the doctor said that it may take a while before I would notice the full effects of my right lung working again.

I finally had everything figured out and the only appointment left for the month was my annual eye exam. I was hoping that later in January, after my follow-up with Iowa City, I would be given the clear for no more doctors' appointments for at least six months.

The eye doctor noticed some leakage in my blood vessels. She said it was odd, because if it had been caused by my diabetes, then both eyes would have been affected. This was only noticeable in my left eye though. I also pointed out that while I had struggled with my diabetes in the beginning, I had done a pretty good job overall of managing it over the years. So that didn't really make sense as an explanation anyway.

She then asked if I had any trauma to my head or upper body, and there it was ... FM strikes again. Remembering that I also had stents in my SVC, she agreed that FM was likely the cause.

I was referred to an eye specialist, who determined the leaking was due to a lack of oxygen to my eyes. I had little vessels that aren't typically there but had developed to try to fix the problem. The body is pretty amazing when you think about it. He said that my body creating these vessels was a good thing, but now they were leaking, so we needed to get them taken care of before they hemorrhaged and caused permanent vision problems. He did state that my left eye was worse; however, my right eye was also showing some damage, so it was decided that I would have surgery on both eyes.

So much for being doctor free for a while.

I was set up to have eye surgery at the end of January, after my follow-up in Iowa City, at the beginning of January.

Tim continued to struggle with his job, trying to stay caught up while I continued to struggle with my health. Both of our tempers were growing, and I was feeling pretty worthless, particularly because I knew my medical expenses were a huge burden on our family. My monthly diabetic expenses alone were pretty hefty, and even though we had insurance, there were still copays for all of the testing and procedures I had been doing. The bills were adding up and we were both frustrated, but I felt responsible. Like it was my fault. I couldn't tell him that though. Instead, I was getting defensive over everything he said.

We continued to go to church every Sunday, and every Sunday, it was like we were the only ones the pastor was talking to. So many of the messages seemed to be directed at us.

One Sunday in particular, he shared a story that I believe he had actually heard from somebody who was talking about things getting so bad that all you can do is "look up." Because God will be there with us and will never leave us.

Every time a new struggle came up with my health, church seemed to be about God giving us opportunities to build our relationships with Him. The particular sermon also focused on being in a valley and how some valleys seemed to go on forever, which I felt was definitely the spot I was at. But the pastor pointed out the verse that said, "Even though I walk *through* the valley of the shadow of death" (emphasis mine), indicating that we will eventually, someday, get out of these valleys.

Almost every Sunday in church consisted of me crying during the sermon. Hearing the pastor talk about situations that Tim and I were dealing with was simply overwhelming. God seemed to be telling us exactly what we needed to hear at the right moments; however, Tim and I were too bitter about our situation to really listen.

On January 10, I went back to Iowa City for a follow-up on my SVC stents. According to Dr. Youness, everything looked great.

Five days later, I went back again for a follow-up on my pulmonary artery stents.

There were four other people from the state of Iowa that were diagnosed with FM from my FM support group. Two of them came to Iowa City for their medical needs, and I knew that Martin, one of the members, was going to be there the same day I was.

The doctor was running behind, but Tim and I had already gotten into a room and were waiting. Tim was standing at the door and looking out when he turned around and told me that he saw Martin in the waiting room. I told him he was wrong, thinking there was no way he could have recognized him from Facebook, but Tim insisted that it was him and kept peeking his head around the door to look. He and I argued back and forth about who should go out and talk to him, as neither of us was overly outgoing, but Tim wound up heading out to introduce himself.

I could hear them talking and I heard Martin say, "Oh, she's here?" So I walked out to introduce myself as well. He shook my hand and the first thing he said was, "Well, you're not on oxygen."

I joked by saying, "Not yet."

Martin and I made some small talk about FM, how we had been diagnosed and how it had affected us. Like me, he had previously been very active, playing football and other sports. The doctors thought he had gotten FM in childhood, though it hadn't presented until he was older.

Martin and I were the same age, although he looked a lot younger. His left lung had been removed, something my doctors were adamantly against because of the calcification and not knowing where all the collateral veins might be. He was wearing an oxygen mask, but otherwise he looked great.

When the doctor finally rounded the corner, I told Martin it had been nice meeting him, and then I went back to the room. It had been another bittersweet moment: so nice to meet a great person who understood what I was going through, but so sad that these had to be the circumstances.

The good news was that my stents were looking great and my right lung was definitely now functioning at 75 percent. I just had to get through my eye surgeries, and I would be good to go.

Ironically, I was more nervous about those eye surgeries than anything else I had had to do in Iowa City. There was just something that really freaked me out about surgery being performed on my eyeball.

As I sat there, anxiously waiting on the day of surgery, Tim decided this was the time to share with me that he had a cow who had only one eye. This cow had recently bumped into him, because the cow could not see. I questioned how this was supposed to help calm my anxiety but could not help but laugh on the inside, imagining the poor, one-eyed cow.

I was called back to the room where they did an eye exam. I bombed that one big time, which Tim graciously decided to point out. He laughed and explained that I shouldn't be nervous about the surgery messing up my eyesight, because I was already blind.

Thanks a lot.

They explained the procedure once again, and then they confirmed they would be working on my left eye, putting a sticker with the letter L above my eye. Again, my loving husband held up his hand to his forehead with the shape of an L and called me a loser. Tim went on to say that the nurses and doctors were out in the hall laughing, because I didn't really need the sticker at all. He said they had just put it on to see if I would really keep it there.

Again, he was full of encouragement and support, and I couldn't help but laugh. This was why I loved him so much. He was very good at knowing when I was upset or in pain by my body language, and he would often throw out a joke to get me to smile.

When my doctor came in, I told him that I had been through a lot of surgeries and procedures before, but that this was, by far, the most bizarre one. The worst part was yet to come, as he proceeded to give me a shot right below my eyelid. It stung with a lot of pressure, and then my eye felt extremely heavy and puffy and I couldn't tell if it was open or shut.

The laser surgery began, and it lasted no more than ten minutes. They put a patch over it and I was sent on my way, knowing I would have to come back the following week for the right eye. I wasn't sure if that was easier or harder—doing only one at a time, knowing exactly what to expect for the next one.

Finally, both eyes were done and I was feeling great, ecstatic that I didn't have to go back to Iowa City until April. That meant no appointments for over two months, which at this point felt like a lifetime.

Every once in a while, someone would ask me about FM. Before the most recent onslaught of surgeries, I routinely felt ashamed or embarrassed to talk about it. Everybody's response was always "You don't look sick." I had gotten so tired of explaining that my looks were deceiving. But now, for whatever reason, I was ready to start sharing about my battle. I was ready to talk about it.

Tim and I stopped at my parents just to say hi after church one day, shortly after finding out that the FM was progressing. My mom called after we left, just to say she couldn't believe how good I was looking on the outside, given how messed up my body was on the inside. We both laughed, because again, it was one of the biggest barriers to understanding this disease.

There were times when I felt uncomfortable complaining about how horrible I felt. Again, it was that underlying fear that people would think I was being dramatic and making things up. I often felt like if I had been carrying around oxygen or looked like I was dying, then maybe everybody else would take the severity of my symptoms seriously.

The reality is that for people who have never dealt with this disease, or seen a family member struggle, truly understanding how serious it can be would certainly be difficult. Even I took years to come to a point of really understanding what I was dealing with—of really being willing to admit to how it would forever affect my life. There were a lot of choices I made along the way that make it clear I wasn't really thinking of this as being the life-threatening illness it is. Sometimes, I am still in denial, and I am the master of excuses. I'm the first to try to pretend that maybe it's really not that bad or that perhaps my symptoms aren't too concerning. I can't always blame others for failing to recognize the severity of this condition, when even I am sometimes hesitant to admit just how bad it is. But I have eight stents in my chest, so obviously something is wrong with me.

Despite how often I may wish that wasn't true.

My health issues were finally improving. The previous six months had been the biggest struggle with FM since I had first been diagnosed, but I was finally feeling good and back to my old self. Because of that, I wanted to appreciate every moment of life that I was able to experience, not taking anything for granted. I had truly seen that tomorrow was never guaranteed.

Unfortunately, the focus had been on my health for so long that Tim and I had failed to recognize just how much our personal life was lacking. We always came back together, despite the many times we took our stress out on each other. I was always able to rely on him. But now, I was determined to start making our relationship a priority again. We needed to find our way back to a happy place, not just a place of survival.

You know what they say about the best-laid plans.

Sunday, January 26, was when everything in our personal life fell down on us. Even though I was finally getting "fixed," the stress had taken its toll. Combined with the medical bills that kept piling up, neither one of us was at our best. After a long day of constant yelling and arguing, Tim and I agreed that we needed to talk with someone, before things got out of control. We were both afraid of things getting to a point where we could not handle our own emotions or repair the damage that was being done. I was finally feeling healthy and alive and was so ready to live life to the fullest. I kept saying how all of my health problems and not being able to control my FM had really made me appreciate absolutely everything in life. But now our relationship was "in the toilet," a reference from one of the recent sermons at our church.

When Tim and I were "on," we were an amazing team. I knew that to be true. But I also knew that when we argued, it could get ugly.

Tim and I contacted Pastor John and explained that our relationship was in crisis and we needed to talk to someone. He set us up to meet with Pastor Gabe at our church.

I just felt sick about everything. I knew that God was not the center of our marriage anymore, and I needed to be looking to Him for peace. The night before we were to meet with Pastor Gabe, I was thinking about everything that I would say. One of the main things I wanted to do was ask Tim for forgiveness for the words that I had said to him.

The day we met with Pastor Gabe, we were able to get to the root of our problems. Tim admitted that he was overwhelmed by our bills, and while he was continuing to expand his business, we still weren't able to keep up. He was working extremely hard, and just when he felt like we might get ahead financially, something else would knock us back down.

Then he took a deep breath in and looked away. He said he didn't know how to say this, because he loved me so much, but he couldn't help but feel that I was an anchor holding him down because of all of my medical expenses.

This was extremely difficult and heartbreaking for me to hear. He cleared his throat, so I knew he was fighting back tears, and he said that of course I was worth it. That he loved me and needed me. But it just felt like when things looked to be getting better, something else was always waiting around the corner. And that something else was often my health.

I looked at him and simply said, "I feel the same way."

And from that point forward, Tim and I slowly began to build our relationship back to where there was more laughing than crying. We still struggled, but now we were able to make a conscientious effort to react the way we wanted to react, turning to God when we needed to get a handle on the situation. We learned to carry on disagreements without raising voices, but it took a lot of conscientious effort to get there.

Pastor John once said in a sermon that we need to look at our own lives to see what story God is writing for us. Shortly thereafter, I began praying for God to show me what story He was writing for me. It was right around the time all of my medical problems began to take over again.

This is why I felt that I needed to share my story. Pastor John also said that nobody is perfect, but our past shows us just how far God has brought us and how good God is. This journey started out in despair, with feelings of hopelessness, loneliness, and defeat. So many times I wanted to give up the fight, yet looking back, God always put the right people or the right song in my life at the most appropriate times.

As much as I tried to stay positive, I often felt defeated, particularly during the times when it felt like we just couldn't catch a break. I felt like I was an inconvenience and a burden to Tim and our families.

While Tim and I have had our struggles, he has gotten me through every depressing and dreadful situation we have encountered by making me laugh. He has been by my side at every appointment and every procedure, and I am forever thankful for that.

For years, I had been crying nearly every Sunday at church. After Tim and I went and spoke with Pastor Gabe, I did not cry the following Sunday. Both Tim and my mom questioned if that meant I had been crying all those years over Tim. I did see how that would appear to be the case, but I assured Tim that he was not the reason. I told him that for the last couple of years, it had seemed like it was one thing right after another in terms of bad news. My health, the loss of our baby, the struggles with Asher when he was first born, then back to my health again. My eyes, my hands, finding out that my FM was actually progressing, sick kids, everyday life, and again, my medical stuff. All of the stress put a lot of strain on our marriage.

I had felt such defeat. When I would fall and start to get back up, something else would come and punch me right back down. It was a recurring theme we were both experiencing. I was such a mess physically, which wore me down mentally. It was hard for me to hide it from my family. Sometimes, I felt like I hadn't even gotten up from my last fall before I would find myself lying on the floor, completely helpless, just taking one blow after the other.

Things had finally started to look up healthwise though. And getting our relationship figured out was one of the last things that I felt we had been struggling with. I had been crying over the years for everything, not just Tim. I wanted him to be happy as well, and I knew that he wasn't. His job overwhelmed him due to how physical and demanding it was. Then my health and not always being able to handle the kids or upkeep our home put extra strain on him. Added to that were the medical expenses and the stress of him worrying about me losing my job, which was where we received our insurance from; it was all just an abundance of everything to take in.

I knew he was stressed, but I also knew he loved and worried about me even more. I always told people I was fine, because

I didn't want to admit that I wasn't able to do the things I once did. I was often stubborn and in denial, and Tim was able to see through that. When I couldn't go on anymore, he was there to encourage me and fight for me. He loved me when I was sick, and he loved me when I was giving up and didn't want to deal with the health problems anymore. He loved me when I would get upset and forgave me for the things that I said to him in moments of stress and fear.

I was beating myself up, feeling like he deserved so much better than me. But he finally assured me of how much he loved me one day by saying, "Our good days outweigh the bad. And the good days are so awesome that I don't want to miss out on them."

When we met, we had both been at points in our lives where we were not living for God. And while I am not proud of some of the things I have done in my past, I also realize now (thanks to those words of one of my favorite pastors) that our pasts show us how great God is by how far we have come. Because of our relationship, I know this to be true.

Whether Tim realizes it or not, he helped me to recognize that my relationship with God was only one sided, as God had given me a new life and all I was doing was taking everything for granted yet again. Tim brought so much light back into my life, and I was finally able to start enjoying the new life I had been blessed with, as well as start to rebuild my relationship with God.

My father-in-law had once told me that Tim's bark is worse than his bite. After five years of marriage, I saw how true that was, as he actually agreed to see Pastor Gabe with me, also proving how deep his love for me, and our family, is. I could see God working through all of this.

That Sunday in church, I did tear up. But where I would have sobbed before, wondering if we would ever get through this, I now had faith that we would. I didn't cry because I finally felt a peace that made it seem as though all of the issues that had been wearing on us the past few years were finally out in the open, getting addressed and taken care of.

FM is a horrible disease. Those of us who have it are affected by it so differently. Every person's experience varies. Even since writing my story, I have had a tremendous amount of new struggles from the effects of what this disease has done to my body. I will continue to have battles with FM for the rest of my life, however long that may be. But as long as I keep God as my main focus, I believe I will be able to get through life with a sincere smile on my face, knowing that I will be okay.

But what do I mean by "okay"?

Because there is no cure and there are limited treatment options, I have finally come to accept what a doctor once told me years ago. The stents that I have are to help improve my quality of life, but this disease will still eventually take that life away. However, I am not giving up the fight. There are days when I cry because I feel so much physical pain, or I am sick of seeing doctor after doctor. It is almost a guarantee that when I go to the doctor for an issue, or even just for a checkup, I will wind up needing some procedure done or will be referred to another specialist for more testing. At times, I get bitter when people make comments about how wonderful it is that I can get a stent to feel better, because they don't understand this is not a cure. Even with my stents open, I will still have good days and bad days. But I try to remember to be thankful for every single day I get, always remembering I have been given more days than I was originally told I would have.

How I feel now is the best I will ever feel, which really isn't so great. I have been trying to be a "success" story with this disease. I want to tell you that I have eight stents, I feel like I did at the age of seventeen, and life is fantastic. I want to say I'm cured and won't have problems anymore. But that is not the case. I did realize while writing my story, however, that while my battle will continue with my physical abilities, I truly am a success story. Because I did not give up or let FM get the best of me.

A lot of people would have thrown in the towel after the initial diagnosis, but I never let this disease have me. I fell in love. I got married. I became a mommy to three more beautiful children. I fought. I struggled. I did what needed to be done to keep living the life I wanted. And I continue to work and love and pray every single day.

Even on the bad days.

Because I do still have bad days where I think about the prognosis and wonder if my time is coming to an end. Then again, there are times when I fantasize about being one of those seventy-year-olds sitting in the waiting room with my oxygen tank. I even have times when I still question if this fight is worth it. But then I push those thoughts out and move on with my life, trying to focus on the amazing positives I have to keep me here.

My husband. My family. And our four amazing kids. Every extra day I get with them is a blessing. I have this incredible extended family that is so full of love and support. There are days where this disease overtakes me and I isolate up in my room, waiting patiently for the pain to subside, not wanting to see or talk to anyone. My mom, of all people, knows if I do not text her back or talk to her that I am having a bad day, but she still texts. As do my other family and friends. Even though I may not respond, that does not mean I don't appreciate the efforts of simply letting me know you are praying for me. So many of my friends and family have reached out to help with meals or the kids as well. And even better, I have so many people praying for me that I don't even know.

I cannot express the gratitude that my family and I have for Dr. Youness and the team of nurses and other doctors and anesthesiologists that I see on a routine basis. I truly am blessed to have so many amazing medical practitioners on my side. They understand this disease and are always looking for solutions to my newest symptoms. But I will forever have a special spot in my heart for Dr. Youness, the first doctor over a five-year span that had any encouraging news for me. The first doctor who told me that I would be around for a long time and to go out and live my life.

At fourteen years old, Skyler is growing into a young lady that I see parts of myself in. I am here to tell her I love her and I am able to experience the arguments with her that every mother should have with her teenager. I am thankful I get to be the one to tell her she can't wear a lot of makeup and that she has to be home right after the dance. I am thankful I get to be the one meeting her friends before she hangs out with them. I am still here to make her flash me looks of disgust because I said no to something, but I am also here to give her the hugs when she needs them. I am here to make her laugh and to have the silly talks and the serious talks. I am here to give her the encouragement that she needs when she is down. I am here to tell her that I love her and I am still here being her mom.

For that alone, I am thankful.

Now looking back, I see how every hurt, every obstacle, and every circumstance led me to something so much better than I could have ever dreamed for myself. While my plan was not working the way I wanted it to, I can look back and see how God's plan for me was playing out. I see how that road trip back home from my brother's is where my relationship with God began to develop again. I now see that my story is not about my disease; it's about a man and a woman who met, fell in love, became a family, and developed a stronger relationship with God.

I want to bring awareness to this horrible disease. We need to find more doctors who are interested in researching it and want to help us to feel better and find a cure. I don't want to be embarrassed to talk about my disease anymore or to shy away when people tell me I look so healthy. Why would anyone think I have a terminal illness that is slowly killing me inside? I have to be willing to speak up, or they will never understand.

I want the next person who is batting FM to make sure they seek out the appropriate doctors who can shed some light on the illness from the start. While those doctors can only admit that FM is a terrible disease to have, and there is not a lot of information to give, they can still encourage and provide hope that there will be help in the future. We need doctors who are not going to discourage us from living our lives or from having that hope.

There will most likely be no cure in my lifetime. But I will do whatever I can to contribute to finding a cure or better treatment options for fibrosing mediastinitis in the future. While it is great that they can treat my symptoms, I want the next person with FM to be able to do so much more than just symptom management.

I have been referred to as a walking miracle, and I believe this to be true. I am proof of the power of prayer. God is good, and I know He has so much more in store for me. Whatever that may be, I will trust in Him, love like no other, and live my life to the fullest.

This is the life I was told I would never live. This is my story.